C000078167

The Spirit of Trees

Fred Hageneder is an author, musician, graphic designer and lecturer whose passion for trees started in his teens. His interests have since extended to comparative religion, cultural history, mythology and archaeology. He is a member of the Ancient Yew Group as well as a co-founder of Friends of the Trees, a charity promoting modern tree sanctuaries. His other publications include *The Heritage of Trees* (Floris Books, 2001) and *The Living Wisdom of Trees* (Duncan Baird, 2005), and his work has been translated into several languages. Born in Hamburg, Germany, in 1962, he now lives in the Cotswolds, England.

Old Beech. *Coloured woodcut by Maxine Relton.*

Fred Hageneder

The Spirit of Trees

Science, Symbiosis and Inspiration

Floris Books

First published in 2000 by Floris Books
Paperback 2006

British Library CIP Data available

ISBN-10 0-86315-557-X
ISBN-13 978-086315-557-4

Produced by Polskabook, Poland

Contents

Acknowledgments

My thanks, firstly, to my parents for encouraging my natural sense of wonder and curiosity. Secondly, to my German publisher Andreas Lentz who has supported my work for a long time, and thanks also to my soul-mate and partner, Vijaya, whose love and patience made this book possible.

The work of Taliesin pen Beirdd inspired me to write this book. One day, I hope to write a tune in his memory. My gratitude to all who took part in the development of the Celtic Tree Circle music, especially Lidia Buonfino, Adam Zablocki, Natasha Czopor, Jan-Peter Klein, and again, Vijaya.

Many thanks to Yvan Rioux for his reflections on natural science, to Christine Konrad for her help with chemistry, and to Norbert Drews for sending me the longest fax I have ever received.

Special credit to my friend Adam Weisberger who taught me that we cannot understand anything without looking at ourselves first, and at the limitations of the observer's perception.

For their professional support in the fields of archaeology and history, I would like to acknowledge: Dr. Alison Sheridan, National Museum of Scotland; Richard Tipping, University of Stirling; Fergus Kelly from the Dublin Institute of Advanced Studies; and, Kenneth Brassil, Nick Walker and especially Robin Gwyndaf from the Museum of Welsh Life. For botany, my thanks to Gordon L. Mackenthun of the Elm Office, and to John Workman, a fourth generation forester. The credit is theirs for what I have managed to get right; if there are errors, the fault is mine.

For the language studies and other research, I would like to mention Eva and Claudius Nenninger, Jörg Wichmann, Dorothea Greve, Nick Macer, and Amanda Isaacs.

Finally, Gloucestershire County Libraries, who helped me to access some rare publications from bygone centuries, and to Amaury Blow for providing a timeless space in which to study them.

Picture Acknowledgments

Dragon Design: page 19 (after Cunliffe); pp. 25, 29 (Creative Collection); pp. 33, 34, 43 (after Rajda); pp. 37, 38 top (after Parkinson, *Introduction to Geomagnetism)*; pp. 38 (bottom), 39 (after Merrill & McElhinny *The Earth's Magnetic Field)*; p. 47 (after *ZeitenSchrift* 14/1977); p. 48 (after Edwards); pp. 31, 50.

Lawrence Edwards, by permission of Floris Books: pages 48, 49.

Fred Hageneder: pages 12, 45, 81, 93, 99, 100, 102, 106, 112, 115, 118, 120, 123, 127, 130, 131, 134, 135, 139, 140, 143, 146, 147, 150, 151, 155, 158 (bottom), 159, 162, 163, 171, 178, 181, 183, 185, 186, 192, 194, 202, 207, 224, 226, 227, 229, 231, 235, 236.

Martin Klatt: pages 119, 124, 166, 191, 215, 218, 219.

Per-Olaf Mademann: pages 27, 159, 174, 179, 198, 203, 210, 218.

Maxine Relton: page 2, 158 (top) (from the private collection of John Ross), 211.

Mrs Steel, (51 Rushton Road, Desborough, Kettering, NN14 2RP): page 46.

Elaine Vijaya: page 82 top (after Bracegirdle & Miles 1971); p. 70 (after Cook 1992); p. 94 (after Stern); p. 71 (after Yarden); pp. 82 (bottom), 84, 85, 86, 87, 92, 95, 104, 141, 164, 190,

H. Wirth (by kind permission of Neue Erde Verlag, Saarbrücken, Germany): page 72.

Dedicated to the soul of the Wildwood

Introduction

Like so many things this book really started with Birch.

As a teenager, a stupid but provocative remark upset me so much that, thinking I could bear life no longer, I set off on my bicycle in search of solitude. I sat down among the scattered birch trees of the wetlands, overwhelmed by despondency. After a while, a movement behind me suddenly caught my attention. I turned around to discover that I was leaning against a young birch tree. My eyes followed its trunk into the sky, and at the same time my soul was lifted too. I tilted my head back and sat with my spine following the gentle movements of the tree swaying in the breeze. As I did so a great sense of peace filled my soul, and my mind was liberated from its emotional cage.

At that moment, I felt as if there were only myself and an invisible power on the Earth, of which the birch tree was a visible representative. I felt that my life could not be beautiful without the existence of something greater and wiser than me. I looked to the tree again and unconsciously surrendered to its divine source of inspiration.

Soon after, my life changed completely, I discovered my talents, my beliefs, my direction and my optimism.

I have always loved nature, but since that day on the moors my relationship with trees became more special. In 1983, I discovered Robert Graves' *The White Goddess* and his Celtic Tree Calendar. I wanted to bring the idea of living with trees through the year to more people, and the result were two Celtic Tree Calendars published in Germany for 1987 and 1988. Each consisted of thirteen black-and-white drawings of trees (a few of which are reprinted in this book), together with brief captions on each tree's role in myth and tradition. The calendars were structured in thirteen moon months of twenty-eight days each, plus an extra day dedicated to the Yew. After two editions, however, I felt that the scope for the artwork was a bit limited, and I also started to feel uneasy about the absence of important trees like Beech or Poplar in the ancient Irish tree alphabet, which was the basis for Graves' calendar. I decided not to produce another calendar before I had solved that mystery.

Many years and trees passed by, the tree calendar question remaining unanswered and almost forgotten, although queries from people wanting a new calendar never really stopped. While on retreat in Ananda Village, Italy, I decided to create a painting and a piece of music dedicated to each

Figure 1.

tree. For two years I worked on music and arrangements for Celtic harp (myself), flute, voice, percussion and some other instruments. When the music was finished in 1995, I realized that it was necessary to present some kind of *introduction* to the tree portraits. When I finally started writing in April 1997 — exactly twenty years after my encounter with the Birch — it was clear that the introduction would need to be some two hundred pages long. It now appears as a large part of this book.

Many customs and the ways in which mankind relates to trees, nature and one another have disappeared since television replaced community life. However, the trees and other natural forces, which originally inspired these customs, are still here. They can inspire us again, to express ourselves and relate consciously to all life forms. This book provides some material, left behind by the wisdom of past generations, as well as fascinating new facts discovered by modern science.

However, this can only be a beginning, for there is so much to be remembered that we have forgotten, and even more that humanity has yet to discover.

PART I

TREES AND
THEIR ENVIRONMENT

1
The Wildwood

If you look at the needle of a compass, you discover that one end always points more or less towards the north, while the other end points south. If you want to explain this, you don't look to the needle but rather to the whole Earth ... The position of the needle cannot be understood unless you know the needle's relationship to the whole Earth.
(Rudolf Steiner 1993, 16)

And so it is with trees ...

Trees are the most successful life forms on Earth. Apart from the oceans, wildwood — mixed woodland of self-sown trees untouched and uncultivated by man — and tropical rainforest form the richest eco-systems in existence, providing a habitat for the widest variety of species. Societies of trees are fundamental to weather and climate, for a beneficial water cycle; for the development of minerals; for balancing the electrical charges between the ionosphere and the Earth's surface; and for the maintenance of the Earth's magnetic field as a whole. In addition, their intelligent and adaptable design, and their ability to co-operate have made trees the dominant life form on Earth since they first appeared more than three hundred million years ago.

This book takes a closer look at the mixed woodlands of the northern temperate zone, as they exist in Europe and North America.

Structure and co-operation

Types of Wildwood

Some trees grow in a wood but not as a wood, such as Holly, while others form woods, like Oak or Beech. Oak dominated the primeval vegetation of Britain, and Beech even more so in Germany. However, it would be a simplification to consider all woods as mere varieties of Oak or Beech. In fact, about two thirds of native trees can predominate locally giving rise to Birch woods, Ash woods, Alder woods, Hazel woods, Lime woods, several sorts of Elm woods and so on. Every wood has its individual peculiarities. Often there is a mixture of roughly a dozen or more trees and shrubs, and in many ancient woods the tree mixture varies in a complex way from one part of the wood to another (Rackham 1976, 32). Soil conditions and climate also play an important role. Thriving Beech stands can be found on chalky ground but also on acidic sands and gravels. This is true for other species too; most temperate species have a wide range of acceptable conditions and are very adaptable.

Succession

Succession is the replacement of one type of vegetation by another, a typical example being acid moorland colonized by Birch, which, in turn, gives way to Oak. Even today, we often see Oak saplings appearing in Birch woods. The reverse is also possible: an old Oak wood is destroyed and the area is subsequently colonized by birch. In the intermediary phases of succession, Ash, Maple and Elm can partly replace Oak and Beech as the dominant species of a woodland. Oliver Rackham, a world authority on trees who teaches botany at Cambridge University, observed woods in West Cambridgeshire, where 'for at least three hundred years the native Ash, Maple and Oak have been slowly and permanently squeezed out by Elm.' The life of the forest — like all of nature — is a peculiar harmony of self-renewing stability on one hand, and constant change and transformation on the other.

Climate

A broadleaved or mixed forest in a temperate climate needs an average temperature of more than 10°C (50°F) for at least six months of the year, and an annual rainfall in excess of 400 mm (16"). The trees' evaporation and assimilation of rain then influences the temperature and humidity of the air. Within a wood the air is always slightly cooler during the day in the warm months, and at night in the cold months it is warmer than the air outside the wood. Amongst the trees, a wide variety of herbal plants, fungi and microbes, as well as insects, birds and wildlife, form part of one of the most complex ecosystems in the world.

Co-operation

Darwin's evolutionary theory regarding competition is nowadays balanced by the discovery of a remarkable amount of interplay and co-operation between life forms. The root systems of plants differ in terms of size, structure and desired nutrients, so that every layer of the soil serves different varieties of plants. Plants co-operate with soil bacteria and fungi, and without this symbiosis there would be no life in the wood, because there would be no wood in the first place. The plants themselves protect each other from wind and extreme weather, and the soil from erosion. The tree roots loosen the soil and maintain its sponge-like consistency. Thus the forest soil becomes a water reservoir for the trees themselves, and for other plants in and around the forest. By shedding their needles or leaves trees share nutrients — which they have gained from the deeper ground layers — with other life forms around them.

Woodland wildlife

In the animal world, too, specializing into niches avoids unnecessary competition. For example, the flycatcher, the great tit and the blue tit all hunt insects in the woods. The blue tit picks insects from the ground, as well as from lower herbs and bushes; the great tit hunts insects in the tree crowns, while the flycatcher hunts in mid-air. Generally when two animals eat similar things, their territories hardly touch, and those whose territories do overlap have different eating habits. In a long period of adaptation the biggest possible number of life forms has made the best use of the habitats and energies of a given area.

Mankind's changes to a landscape have a strong influence on biodiversity. Even the European primeval forest did not possess the greatest variety of animal and plant species, as it covered vast areas in a rather uniform way. Instead it was a certain stage of man-made landscape. Following the exploitation of the Middle Ages the European woodlands recovered — aided by the intervention of the Black Death and the Thirty-Year-War. The woods were replaced by a multitude of different landscapes: parkland meadows, pasture woods, clearings, recovering wastelands, drying wetlands, Birch groves, Oak forests, Hazel woods, Beech forests, Willow copses, and many more. During the last two centuries, the conversion from this rich diversity to conifer monocultures destroyed the habitats of many species. However, farming and other human activities also create new habitats for animals and birds, at the edges of woods or elsewhere.

Trees and fire

Bushfires and lightning fire have a history that is as old as vegetation. In natural cycles, fire is not necessarily destructive. A forest that has become too old can actually be rejuvenated by the effects of fire. Ashes increase the alkaline quality of the soil and new plants start to grow. For many plants, fire kills their parasites and competitors. The seeds of certain plants lie dormant for years and are awakened by the changes fire brings in light, soil acidity and warmth. Healthy old trees generally survive forest fires.

The impact of fire on the Wildwood changed drastically when the human race started to use fire. Rudimentary forms of tool use and language are found among other animals, but the use of fire is exclusively human.

It is not known when man's control over fire started. Excavations on African sites from 1,400,000 years ago are controversial, but solid evidence has been found that *Homo erectus* was using fire in various parts of Europe and Asia at least 400,000 years ago; long before *Homo sapiens* — modern man — appeared.

The task of maintaining a fire and handing it down from generation to generation brought about enormous changes for the human population. Gathering wood and storing it during wet periods is not part of the genetic code, it had to be learned.

Adding the power of fire to their own, early societies became more productive and more powerful, resulting in increased material comfort, security and population. In the history of evolution, no human groups without fire survived; those with fire ascended to ecological dominance.

All human civilization and culture has been built — and still is — on the use of fire and wood. Trees provided their very bodies to cushion humanity's development. Everywhere it went humankind could only survive because trees had come before them. This direct reliance on trees has been the longest dependency in the cultural history of humankind.

Trees and ice

During an ice age, glaciers, caused by global cooling, begin to move down towards the valleys, eventually forming gigantic ice sheets that spread over vast areas of the Earth's surface, with a possible height of 3,000m (10,000 feet). With the cooling down of the climate all life had to retreat southwards — including trees, that also survived the Ice Ages through migration.

Since these global temperature changes happened over thousands of years, each species had time to slowly move southward, following their most favourable weather conditions. In Europe, there was, however, one problem: the European mountains — the Pyrenees, the Alps and the Carpathians — which run from west to east, and thus blocked the migratory routes. The Mediterranean Sea formed a similar barrier. Many tree, plant and animal species did not manage to bypass these blockades and became extinct. Time and again — there have been at least four, probably even more, ice ages — the flora and fauna had to make their way south and back again.

In North America, where the mountain chains run in a north-south direction, tree species were not blocked in the same way. Therefore, America now has about seventy-two species of Oak while Europe has less than half that number. The same is true for many other trees, particularly conifers.

An Ice Age leads to a subsequent period of renewal for a landscape. Only those species, which could adapt to the changed soil and climate conditions, survived. The trees that returned by their own resilience and adaptability is thus the group considered to be truly *indigenous* to a particular area.

The return of the European trees has been carefully examined. When the climate warmed up and the ice sheets slowly began to melt (from 12000 BC onwards), some sparse vegetation developed, and was slowly joined by more prolific plants and finally by the mixed Wildwood which, in various forms, had existed in Europe before for countless millions of years.

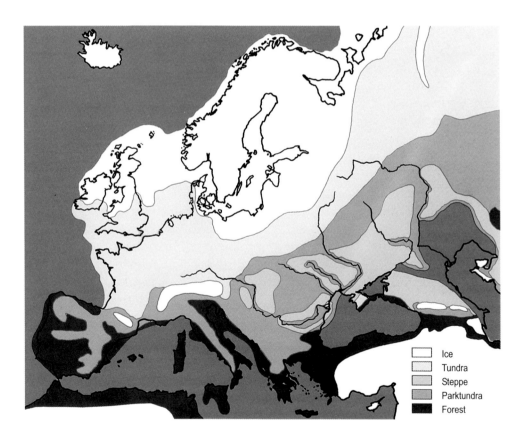

Ice
Tundra
Steppe
Parktundra
Forest

Figure 2. Map of Europe at the peak of the last Ice Age (c. 16000–18000 BC). The extended coastlines are due to the lower sea level, as a lot of water was confined within the ice. Note also how far south the Wildwood retreated.

The first tree to appear in the wet wastelands and the grassy tundra was Birch, at the beginning of the tenth millennium BC (Milner 1992, 72; Stern 1979, 76). Pine *(Pinus sylvestris)* followed shortly afterwards, its woods sometimes replacing, sometimes alternating with those of Birch. Poplar and Willow were Birch's early companions in the wetlands, while the rare Juniper preferred the open steppe, and patches of Rowan mainly appeared along hillsides. The seeds of the latter two were not carried by wind as those of the others, but by the birds, who were also returning.

The migration routes of trees generally pointed north but with very different tendencies depending on the species. For example, the British Isles were repopulated by Birch in a clear east-to-west direction, taking about two thousand years for this tree to reach Ireland from its refuge areas in the Mediterranean. Pine on the other hand came south-north, taking 1,500 years to reach the Scottish border, although it took more than twice as long to spread over the Highlands. Many trees reached their latitudinal and/or altitudinal limits in this geographical area. The wet and peaty conditions also created further obstacles for the trees' distribution (Tipping 1994, 11f).

During the Middle Stone Age (8000–2700 BC) the climate became warmer still, inviting more species. About a thousand years later, Hazel appeared around the shores of the Irish Sea, and then spread westwards over Ireland, but eastwards over Scotland and England. It is assumed today that this was influenced by the expansion of human populations, which re-populated many areas at about the same time. Elm came back with Oak, soon joined by Holly which favours Oak's presence. Yew returned to the post-glacial chalky grounds and Alder repopulated the wetlands.

In the sixth millennium BC, the climate became even warmer — an average 3°C (37.5°F) warmer than today — allowing Ash, Hawthorn and Lime (or Linden) to return. A long period of relative stability began.

By 3000 BC, the Norway Spruce *(Picea abies)* was re-established in the mountainous areas. Its post-glacial appearance in Scandinavia, Russia and the Baltic is due to its retreat to Middle Russia, while central Europe was colonized from two other areas — the foot of the Carpathians (modern Romania) and Slovenia. Although Spruce is a tree armed for the cold, it took a very long time to spread again. This is perhaps because it could not simply *jump* between mountainous regions, and was unable to push through the flat, and wet, lands, which were the domain of other species which were better able to cope with the lowland conditions. For example, it never naturally reached northern Germany; Spruce only gained a strong foothold in the Black Forest in south Germany two thousand years ago.

The tree with the most astonishing distribution history is Beech. It took a very long time to return and another vast period to gain dominance over the mixed Oak woodlands. About 2000 BC Beech spread over Germany and France, but it remained a rare tree in the British Isles, only becoming more widespread later, following human settlement. Beech still has no real significance in Ireland, and its scarcity in parts of Germany, Holland and the British Isles is further evidence of its late and incomplete return. However, it did succeed in transforming large parts of Europe into Beech landscapes — mixed with Ash, Sycamore and Elm.

Thus the Wildwood reclaimed Europe.

2
The Cradle of Water

The waters of life

Ken Jordan, a chemist and water researcher at the University of Pittsburgh, said that many questions about the essential and, in many respects, mysterious substance — water — are still unanswered. Nobody understands, for example, why water can store so much warmth (Kneissler 1997, 10). Paul Caro, the internationally renowned chemist and Director of Research at the French National Scientific Research Centre (CNRS), adds in his book, *Water:*

> We can measure the varied properties of water over a wide range of temperatures, yet the measurements reveal that water acts like a strange substance that defies logic. Is water "abnormal?"— Scientific thinking on this question is divided.

During a seminar in 1991, the German physicist and water engineer, Wilfried Hacheney, stated:

> To this day it cannot be explained why water is liquid. All known natural laws and their functional structures do not hold for water.

What is so troublesome about water? Here are just a few of its *abnormalities*:

— Water boils at 100°C (212°F), but the water molecule is so small that according to theoretical science it should turn from fluid to steam at –75°C (–103°F). Why then is water a fluid?
— According to the Periodic Table water's freezing point should be –120°C (–184°F) instead of 0°C (32°F).
— When frozen it expands instead of shrinking, and also floats.
— Its surface tension is ten times higher than theory expects.

Of all known substances water is unique in the way it eludes the systems of intellectual science. 'It is exactly the extraordinary qualities of water that are the foundation of development and preservation of life on this planet' (Hacheney 1991).

The scientist and inventor, Viktor Schauberger, said water is a 'living organism with its own laws' (Alexandersson 1990).

Nearly three quarters of the Earth's surface is covered with water. Similarly a human being is 60–75 per cent water — 70 per cent of our brain consists of water, 92 per cent of our blood and 99 per cent of all our metabolic processes are dependent on it. After examining living and dying blood cells (erythrocytes), the Austrian biophysicist, Karl Trincher, concluded: 'The actual basis of life is the inter-cellular water and not the biological macro-molecules ... The secret of life lies in the water' (Arndt, August 1996, 19).

One of the secrets of water is its ability to form special macro-molecules, so-called *clusters*. Water molecules (H_2O) have a tendency to socialize. Owing to their particular shape and electrical charges water molecules link up via hydrogen (H) bridges, thus forming large groups of hundreds of molecules.

It has been discovered that this ability to form clusters is used to encase other molecules, such as sugars, salts, proteins, acids or poisons. The water molecules completely enclose the other molecule, thereby making a copy of its shape. When the other molecule is filtered out, these clusters retain a perfect imprint of the 'guest' — and moreover, they carry its *vibrational* frequency and information.

In science, water is increasingly credited with possessing a memory. Indeed, the gigantic number of possible variations of these geometrical cluster shapes could fill whole libraries with information. The complexity of events in water is so vast that, in 1997, the most powerful computing systems — for example, at the National Centre for Supercomputing in Illinois or at the Pittsburgh Supercomputing Centre, where such calculations were run — could only calculate the possible interactions of just eight water molecules (Kneissler 1997).

Crystal water

Water arranges its clusters in even bigger groups which take the form of the five Platonic bodies: the tetrahedron, the cube, octahedron, dodecahedron, and icosahedron. In Classical times, these were associated with divine energies and proportions, as well as with cosmic forces (planets).

Water clusters have complex and stable structures, which are maintained

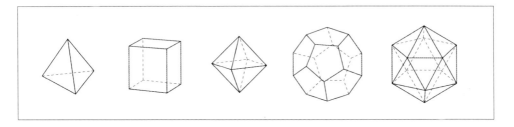

Figure 3. The Platonic bodies are the only five bodies which consist of regular polygons meeting at the same angle.

in steam and bound by a very strong energy bond. Their degree of order is more akin to crystals — which have the highest order currently known about. Thus, water clusters are called *fluid crystals*.

These crystal water structures vibrate with high frequencies and send out a whole range of signals. They are also considered to be antennae for the reception of signals.

Water has a tendency to cool down towards its *anomaly point* of +4°C (39°F). At this temperature its physical density is at its highest. The closer the temperature is to +4°C (39°F) the more complex the clusters become (between 300 and 400 molecules per cluster at 37°C (99°F), but up to 700 at +4°C (39°F). Therefore the information density of the water is also at its highest.

Below +9°C (48°F) oxygen no longer promotes the life of micro-organisms such as bacteria. Therefore, staying cool provides a hygienic environment as well as increased information density. Running streams always try to shade themselves, and for this they have a powerful ally: the forest.

The cycle of water

Water molecules in the ionosphere (the Earth's atmosphere above 80 km/50 miles) absorb light and other high frequency energies from the Sun and other cosmic sources. In 1962, the double Nobel prize winner, Linus Pauling (then Director of the Physio-Chemical Institute at the University of Berkeley), discovered that in the extreme cold at 100–150 kilometres (60–100 miles) above the Earth, water does not freeze! The perfectly round droplets are 7.4 times more stable than mercury.

When rain falls it absorbs atmospheric oxygen, nitrogen and other gases, and also charges electrically and magnetically. Part of this charge together with the gases are passed on to plant leaves through physical contact. This makes rain vitally important for the plant world.

The water reaches the ground and soaks through the cool earth. The redundant oxygen feeds the multitude of micro-organisms that are a crucial part of any healthy soil. Sinking into deeper layers the water cools down towards its anomaly point (+4°C/39°F). Deep in the soil various chemical reactions — particularly with magnesium, calcium and carbon dioxide — split the hydrogen and the oxygen and later, bind these elements together again, creating new water. This water does not carry old information patterns and is absolutely pure. It begins to rise and on its way absorbs information and substances from the mineral world.

This *juvenile* water is sterile, distilled and devoid of so-called *impurities*. It has no developed character and qualities and, therefore, absorbs the characteristics and properties of whatever it comes into contact with, such as trace elements, minerals, salts and even smells! Were we to just drink pure water, it would quickly leach out our store of minerals and trace elements, debilitating and ultimately killing us. This is why spring water is so much healthier than pure water, which has been pumped directly from its source, as spring water has had time to complete its natural absorption process.

Trees in the cool forest absorb water from the soil and cool the soil's upper layers. The laws of physics dictate that cold water is not found above warm water, so the new water rises towards the surface. Forests keep the ground water table high and also contain many springs. Here in the cool, diffused light of the forest the water begins its long, life-giving cycle, winding its way towards the valleys, always shaded by green foliage. As long as it can, water avoids the harmful direct light of the Sun by shielding itself under overhanging vegetation. Conceived in the cool, dark cradle of the forest water transports its vital energies, minerals and trace elements to other environments and, ultimately, to the sea, from where clouds are born. And so the cycle continues.

The forest — cradle of water

Some of the *young* water is absorbed by the vegetation. The tree makes use of the temperature differences to do this — during the day the inside of the tree is cooler than the air, and at night the tree is warmer than the air. Thus, in the daytime water rises easily into the crown. When crown and trunk cool down the roots warm up and vice versa. In effect the ground is kept warm at night and in the winter, and kept cool in the day and during the summer. This stabilization of soil temperature is vitally important for micro-organisms.

A lot of the tree's water is lost through the tiny stomata in the leaves and

Figure 4. Pool in the woods by Per-Olaf Mademann.

rises through the atmosphere. At a height of three to four kilometres (2–3 miles) above the ground it starts its cycle again.

By absorbing large amounts of water from the soil the tree also extracts warmth from the soil. Water is pulled upwards from the deeper layers of the ground and cools as it nears the surface. A balanced water table is therefore influenced and maintained by the water metabolism of trees. Viktor Schauberger stated:

> Without a healthy forest, there can be no healthy water, no healthy blood. (Alexandersson 1990).

Every tree is a water column, which constantly supplies the air with moisture. The clear-felling of whole forests results in an inevitable change in regional climate. The water table sinks and the land becomes barren.

Schauberger uses the example of a mountain spring in Salzkammergut, Austria (Alexandersson 1990).The water was highly charged and rich in trace elements, and it did not freeze in the winter. The colder the air, the warmer the water was: at −30°C (−22°F) the water had a temperature of up to +10°C (50°F). However, on very hot summer days the water temperature came close to the anomaly point of +4°C (39°F). During World War I, clear-felling operations were carried out 600–800 metres (2000–3000 feet) below the spring. The following year the spring began to dry up. The rare herbs and tall grasses that had flourished around it disappeared. Next, the chamois, which drank from the spring became ill, and mange, a disease rarely found in that area, wiped them all out. The only surviving small groups of chamois lived near to similar springs. According to Schauberger, they needed the highly charged water to charge their blood in order to live at such Alpine heights.

However, the trail of suffering does not stop with the disappearance of springs. Brooks flowing through clear-felled wasteland lose their temperature balance and become raging torrents. Natural brooks do not destroy their bed nor do they flood, even after heavy downpours, but by removing the forest brooks can no longer keep their beds clean. The water's current, weakened by over-heating, increasingly fails to transport sediments from the bottom of the riverbed, and fills up with stones and mud. The flow forces, which naturally concentrate the movement of the water towards the centre of the stream, are diverted to the outside and undermine and destroy the riverbanks. Artificial measures, embankments and straight linear channels only worsen the situation. Forcing water to flow in an unnatural, straight line only accelerates its degeneration. The vegetation-less riverbanks and the surrounding, eroding wastelands add even more water to the damaged riverbed. Man, therefore, broadens the channel, thereby exposing even more water to the Sun's heat. The vicious circle goes on ...

According to Viktor Schauberger, water subjected to these conditions loses its character, its soul; it becomes increasingly violent and aggressive as it casts about seeking to vent its anger and restore to itself its former health and stability (Coats 1998, 7). The chaos widens and natural disasters like catastrophic floods haunt the valleys and the deltas, while deforested mountains become uninhabitable because of avalanches and landslides.

In the lower reaches of the Danube, for example, 'almost a million hectares of valuable farmland have been lost due to the regulation of the upper reaches' (Coats 1998, 17).

In 1930, Viktor Schauberger, also stated: 'Without the forest, no water; without water, no bread; without bread, no life' (Alexandersson 1990).

We possess the knowledge of how to create and maintain a balanced life for forest, water and humankind, but the responsible social organs — governments, districts, experts, companies — still repeat the mistakes of the past. If we do not change our ways very soon we will be forced to do so by the sheer pressure for survival.

As Julian Jones, a water management consultant, states in a personal comment:

> Aquarius is the age of the water bearer, the age when we humans will discover and apply the natural secrets of water, by thus lifting (bearing) water to a higher level, a healed and restored world will come into being.

Figure 5. Water droplet.

3
Trees, Electricity and Magnetism

Electricity and magnetism are two phenomena of electromagnetism associated with the fields and forces of charge. They were long thought to be separate forces until Albert Einstein's Theory of Relativity, in 1905, established beyond doubt that they are both aspects of one thing. Electrical and magnetic forces are found in regions called electrical and magnetic fields, which are fundamental in nature, and can exist far from the charge which generates them, and travel through space as electromagnetic radiation waves. Radio and television waves, microwaves, infra-red, gamma and X-rays, ultraviolet and visible light, all belong to the electromagnetic spectrum (see below), and travel with the velocity of light (roughly 298,000 km/186,000 miles per second) Their only difference is the wavelengths in which their fields vibrate.

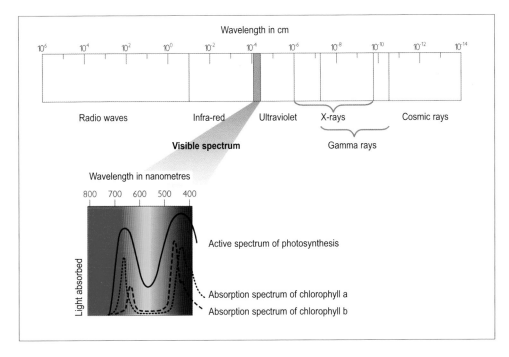

Figure 6. The electromagnetic spectrum and light absorption by plants. Chlorophyll reacts mainly to the edges of the visible spectrum, and less so to the green centre.

Electrical forces are produced by electrical charges either in rest or in motion. Magnetic forces, on the other hand, are produced only by moving charges and act solely on charges in motion ... Electrical fields can produce magnetic fields and vice versa. (*Encyclopaedia Britannica*)

Electrical events occur everywhere because the electrical charge is incorporated in atoms and is thereby responsible for most of the physical and chemical properties of all atoms and molecules. The physical bodies of trees like those of humans are electromagnetic phenomena.

Electricity and vitality

The Swiss electro-technician and electrotherapist, Eugen Konrad Müller, (1853–1948) proved the electrical potential of the human body and its correlation with weather, moods, physiological events, nutrition and temperature. In 1925, he observed the electrical currents of a Sycamore, measuring the 'electrical life activities' of the tree with a galvanometer (an instrument for measuring low electrical currents), which was connected to a photographic device.

A few years later, a leading American neuro-anatomist at Yale, Harold Saxton Burr, performed extensive surveys of the electro-dynamic force fields of living organisms. He showed that each species and subspecies of plant has its own pattern, its own characteristic, constant and relatively invariable potential difference. Between 1943 and 1966, he recorded the bio-electrical fields of an Elm and a Sycamore every hour, thus proving for the first time that trees possess a bio-electrical field, and that:

— Tree potentials vary from 0 to 500 mV (millivolts).
— Trees show a daily rhythm with a minimum in the early morning and a maximum in the afternoon.
— Trees show an annual rhythm with a minimum in April and a maximum in September. The turning points in the annual rhythm are the equinoxes.
— The bio-electrical field of trees reacts sensitively to physiological activities, changes of light and darkness, and to air electricity and changes in the Earth's magnetic field.
— The bio-electrical fields react to the phases of the Moon, as well as to the main solar cycle, which takes about eleven years.

An extensive series of field studies between 1989 and 1990, by the Czech scientist, Vladimir Rajda, revealed that the measurement of trees' geo-phyto-electrical currents (GPEC) made it possible to determine the health of trees with great precision. This is because electrical currents reflect the bio-chemical metabolism of the tree so closely that the two phenomena can be understood as a *biophysical unity*.

The electrical currents also show a direct biophysical connection with electrical currents in the soil, as well as with air electricity, electromagnetic waves from the Sun and planets, and changes in the Earth's magnetic field. The characteristics of the electrical currents do not show the usual correlations with external environmental factors, as their source seems to be the living being itself. This led Rajda to the assumption that plants are capable of auto-regulating their electrical currents. One aspect of this biological independence is the fact that each tree species shows individual characteristics.

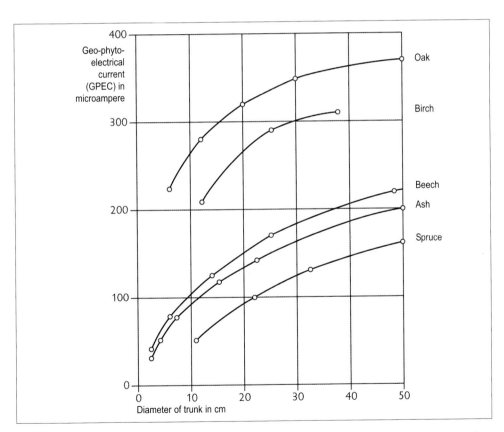

Figure 7. The electrical currents in phloem and cambium layers of various tree species, measured continually between 1969 and 1989 at the base of the trunk. (From Rajda 1992).

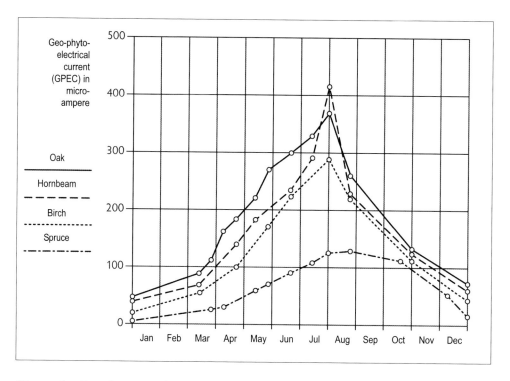

Figure 8. Regular annual variations in the GPEC of Oak, Hornbeam, Birch and Spruce. At the beginning of August, the evergreen shows a smaller rise than the other trees. (After Rajda 1992).

Long-term studies have demonstrated that the electrical currents of trees of one species have the same annual rhythm, modified only by differences in age, dimensions and soil quality. Generally, an increase in light raises electrical currents, especially in trees exposed to a lot of light, such as Birch trees. Air temperature has a similar effect — 1°C (1.8°F) equals a GPEC intensity change of 2.8 microampere. However, these external factors alone are not sufficient in explaining the variance in the electrical activities of different plant species.

The electrical currents form an energetic bridge between the inorganic nutrients of the soil and living plants. The optimum supply ensures perfect health, resistance, and growth. A damaged tree, on the other hand, reveals a significant decrease in the intensity of electrical current *before* any visual signs of illness appear. This is then followed by a decrease in water uptake and nutrient supply. The electrical currents decrease further, while the electrical resistance of the tree increases enormously. The balanced distribution of plant nutrients collapses. For example, in Oak, there is a deficiency of magnesium, potassium, nitrogen, calcium, copper, zinc and phosphorus, while manganese can be found in excess. Following a long period of under-nourishment the tree is too weak to keep parasites at bay.

Rajda actually managed to heal plants with medium damage by raising their electrical currents back to normal levels — with the help of car batteries! However, exact control is necessary, as exceeding the natural maximum value of a species — as reached in high summer (see figure) — will directly damage or destroy plant organs.

In this context 'tree hugging' no longer seems so ridiculous. A person's physical distance from the electrically active layers of xylem and phloem is only a few centimetres at most, sometimes only a few millimetres. Real energy exchange is actually inevitable.

Electricity and growth

In the mid 1970s, physiological plant research in the Soviet Union proved that apart from light, temperature, moisture and nutrition, photosynthesis is dependent on a fifth external factor — the electrical charge of the air.

Earth's surface has a negative electrical charge, while the ionosphere is positively charged. In good weather, the tension voltage between Earth and the ionosphere is about 300,000 V/m at its strongest. The electrical field of air usually reaches 100–120 V/m in valleys. As the conductivity of the air increases with height the voltage decreases accordingly to about 4 V/m at an altitude of 10 km (7 miles). The Russian surveys showed that the photosynthesis of plants is stimulated by an increasingly negative charge of the soil, but slows down with the charge inversion present during thunderstorms. (Storm clouds have a strong negative charge on their lower side, which forces the Earth below to take on a positive charge.)

Plants are electrical conductors because of their sap flow. Trees continually discharge the air electrical tension voltage between the Earth and the ionosphere, which is seen by their function as lightning conductors. However, even in good weather the air's electrical field can be too high for plants and can damage them through *point discharges* (miniature lightning strikes occurring on the leaf or twig, which are invisible to the human eye).

Point discharges at the tops of trees occur from 600 V/m upwards, causing an electrical current of 10^{-6} ampere. Height and solitary position increase the likelihood of such discharges considerably. Therefore trees of 30 m (100 feet) or more attract point discharges even in good weather and in valleys. 'In heavy showery precipitation the field strength can increase to 10,000 V/m, which brings about corona discharges on tree tops like in a thunderstorm.' (Fischer 1993, 648). In mountain areas such discharges can even occur on the tops of blades of grass (Chalmers 1953, 346f & 1955, 149–159; Whipple & Scrase 1936).

According to the magnetic field research scientist, Rainer Fischer, the air's electricity is a crucial factor for the tree line in mountains. The water flow in the xylem makes use of attractive electrical forces for the transport of nutrients. Since the air's conductivity is much stronger at high altitudes electrical currents and the discharge of air electricity are also more intense than in the valleys. *Cations,* which constitute the major part of tree nutrients, are therefore held back in the soil and cannot rise with the water, a situation that leads to serious deficiencies in the tree (see Botanical Basics, pages 81–96).

Maintaining the Earth's magnetic field

Trees are not only occasional lightning conductors but continuously discharge air electricity. Every electrical conductor creates an electromagnetic field around itself while an electrical current flows through it. The electromagnetic fields of trees are rather weak, but not insignificant. According to the laws of Physics the electromagnetic fields of electrical conductors amplify each other when they are parallel, and have currents running through them in the same direction. This applies to trees as well, and many billions of trees participate in creating and maintaining the Earth's magnetic field. Our planet is the only solid one within the solar system with a real magnetic field, apart from Mercury which has an extremely weak one. Rainer Fischer, who discovered these relationships in 1986, says:

> The electromagnetic fields of huge forests affect the outer core of the Earth, which has a very high electrical conductibility. Through the tidal drag of the Earth's crust the core spins somewhat faster. The electromagnetic influence of the forests is conducted through magnetic fields in the core where it induces electrical currents, thus in turn creating magnetic fields. In this way the vegetation has a charging effect on the Earth's magnetic field, orientated to the geographic pole. This becomes evident by the correlation between the density of vegetation and the declination of the Earth's magnetic field. The declination, or deviation between the magnetic pole and the rotation pole, should theoretically be a simple, mathematically calculable figure. But in reality it is very different from that. What is noticeable is that in the great forests of the earth, the deviation is zero, the compass needle pointing to true north. (Fischer 1994).

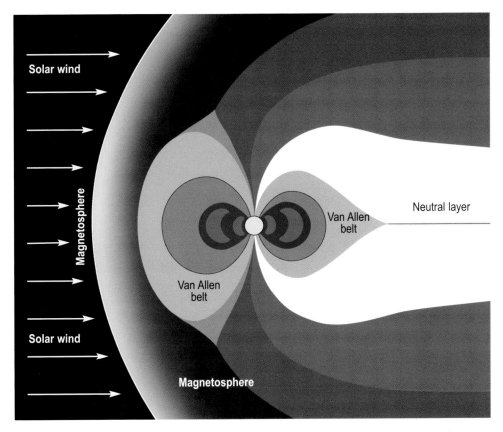

Figure 9. The Earth's magnetic fields. Above the poles there are deep gorges in the magnetic field where the greatest amount of cosmic radiation enters, some of which is visible as the northern lights.

Science previously had no sufficient explanation for what sets the electrical currents in motion in the first place. Again Fischer:

> Many theories have been developed to answer this question. But the simplest, the electromagnetic effect of countless parallel vegetable electrical conductors has been overlooked completely. (*Trendwende* 1987, 1–2, 1)

> The strength of the Earth's magnetic field is dependent on the density of the vegetation. When the vegetation retreats the magnetic field strength of the Earth decreases. Today, exactly this is revealing itself to a high degree (*Trendwende* 1987, 3–4, 2)

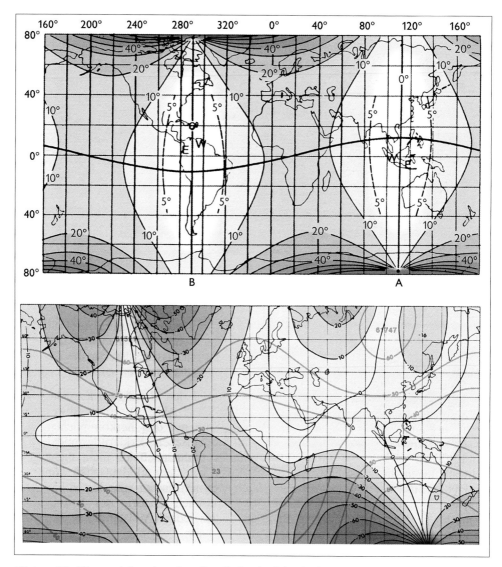

Figure 10. Theory (above) and reality (below) of the declination in the Earth's magnetic field.

Previous theories of Earth's self-maintaining magnetic field contain central contradictions. A simple law of physics states that every magnet has its highest intensity at its poles and its lowest at its Equator, but this is not the case with Earth.

— The point of highest intensity in the northern hemisphere is presently located more than 1,500 miles (2,500 km) south of the magnetic pole, above the last extensive forest areas of Canada.

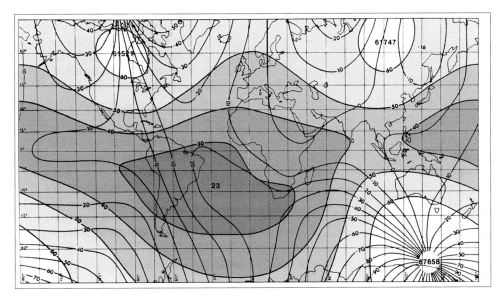

Figure 11. Regions of total intensity of the Earth's magnetic field.

— The northern hemisphere possesses a second point of even higher intensity, again above large woodlands in Siberia. Only in Antarctica, where
hardly any vegetation occurs near the South Pole, do magnetic pole and
highest intensity meet.
— Lowest total intensity is then expected at the Equator. It does not occur
above the tropical rain forests, but at a latitude of 35°S where most continents and their vegetation end.

Continuous examinations report a drastic decrease in the strength of the
Earth's magnetic field that parallels global deforestation. Since measurements began in 1838, total global intensity has dropped by ten per cent. A
decrease of just one per cent can cause an increase in neutron radiation at
sea level of two per cent, and at high altitudes of four per cent.

With the clear-felling of woodlands Man is bringing about the decline of
the Earth's magnetic field which, with the magnetosphere, creates the
planet's only effective protective shield against hard particle radiation from
the Sun and the cosmos.

4
Light and Colour

Light and growth

Light, magnetism and electrical energy are all different forms of the same energy. The differences lie in their vibration rates and transmitting substances. Any of these energy forms can be transformed into another.

Light is essential for the nutrition, growth and reproduction of plants. Like all matter and radiation, light has both a wave and a particle aspect.

Almost all plants need light and water for their metabolism, but not every plant needs the same amount of light and intensity. In a forest light sensitive plants grow sheltered on the inside, while the forest borders are protected by plants which are less sensitive.

The Birch is protected by reflective shiny white bark, and can therefore colonize bright open moorland or venture into hills and mountains, with a high level of ultraviolet light.

Blackened trees, which have survived a forest fire, overheat too easily in these environments, because black is the most efficient colour at absorbing all light frequencies and thermal radiation. Some species are able to produce new shoots all along their trunk to make good use of the increased light intensity and to shade and cool the trunk. The temperature of a tree increases with an increased exposure to light and warmth.

Light significantly influences the tree's growth pattern. Trees enjoying sufficient amounts of light from all sides can develop a broad crown with branches closer to the ground, while dense forest results in narrow crowns and relatively slender trunks.

Colour

Colour, in the form of light, makes up part of the electromagnetic spectrum. The colours visible to the human eye have wavelengths between 385 and 760 nanometres (1 nm = one millionth of a millimetre). The wavelengths of ultraviolet light are between 100 and 385 nm. Any wavelengths longer than 760 nm denote infra-red light, which blends into thermal radiation (see Figure 6). All forms of light, X-rays and electro-magnetic fields have strong and various effects on living bodies.

Plants and animals have many things in common, such as respiration as well as the kind of light they dwell in, and therefore complement each other. Humans need light and colours as well as air, water and food, and the frequencies humans thrive on are what are known as the *visible* part of the spectrum: from red via orange, yellow, green and blue to purple. Green is the most intense. Trees are insensitive to green light and work more with the ends of the spectrum: red to infra-red, and violet to ultra-violet.

The human body absorbs light through the eyes, skin and food. The reactions of the retina have a vital effect on the whole nervous system, stimulating many biological processes. For example, the frequency of processes in the cerebral cortex relies on the brightness of absorbed colours. A form of light is also present in the transmission of impulses through the nervous system. The skin can select colours, filter the available spectrum, and pass required frequencies on to the body. If exposed to a continuous flood of strong light the skin's pores close. The DNA of any animal or plant can also store light.

Plants breathe in carbon dioxide for photosynthesis, which uses red and yellow light. Without these plant abilities no animal life (including human life) could exist on Earth.

The *body colour* of objects results from certain interactions between radiation energy and matter. Molecular structures (matter) absorb certain frequencies (colours) from the spectrum and reflect others. A black object absorbs all of the radiation energy, a shining white object reflects it all. A green leaf absorbs the red part of the spectrum for the assimilation of carbon dioxide, and reflects the green.

However, no current light theory can fully explain the whole phenomenon. Plants grown exclusively under green light should, in theory, not be able to absorb any light and should therefore wither and die. However, experiments with lettuce showed that the plants grew even more successfully under green glass than in direct sunlight (Amber 1983, 37f).

Since green is the dominant colour of the forest, the physio-psychological effects of green light rays on human beings are of interest. Green is situated in the middle of the colour spectrum, which is reflected by its effects. In chromotherapy (colour healing) green is known to cool, soothe, calm and relax, both physically and mentally. Green is also associated with energy, youth, growth, fertility, hope and new life.

Biophotons

The smallest amounts of light are called *quantums* or *photons*. Biophotons are particles (waves) of light emanating from living cells.

Biophoton radiation is very weak, and invisible to the human eye. Biophoton radiation is caused by electrically stimulated molecules within the body, often as a result of light absorbed by the organism, but also caused by electromagnetic waves, warmth or sound.

Light can be found in all living vegetable or animal cells. It has a high degree of order, a stable intensity and is constant, without the fluctuations of normal light — it is like biological laser light. Its coherence is far higher, even more perfect, than that of technically produced laser light.

Owing to its high degree of order a biophoton field can direct other structures towards order and transmit information, which seems to be its purpose; the field of coherent radiation is the central regulation factor of the cell. Since all cells of an organism — such as a tree or person — are

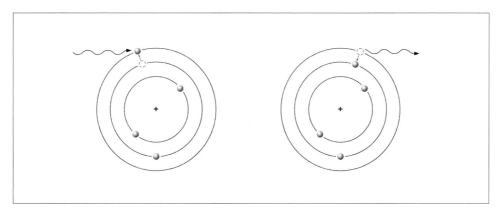

Figure 12. Interaction of light and matter.
Left: A light photon hitting an atom can in certain cases cause an electron to be lifted from its orbit to an outer orbit that has a higher energy level (quantum leap).
Right: After a moment of stimulation the electron jumps back into its rest orbit, and the photon is emitted again.

connected, the whole organism has a shared field of biophotons that navigate the life processes. Signals — for example, to activate or reduce biochemical processes, create tissue, or fight intruders or poisons — can be sent with the speed of light to any part of the body.

Absorption experiments have shown that biophoton emission can travel through thousands of living cells with hardly any loss; plant shoots can channel weak light inside themselves without loss.

Plant and animal tissue are light-transmissive, but at the same time cells are able to absorb the information when they require. Cells can also retain light and release it later, through natural decay, and at a different frequency. The secret lies in DNA.

Light and DNA

The essential store and transmitter for cellular biophoton emission is the DNA in the nucleus, from where at least seventy-five per cent of the emission originates. The DNA molecule is able to absorb and transmit light through rhythmical contractions. This discovery has led to the conclusion that the DNA molecule network controls the biophoton field of the organism, through co-operation with a hierarchy of light-active molecules. These structures literally work like aerials; their geometry and dimensions have evolved with the biophoton field, within terrestrial and cosmic radiation fields, to work in perfect harmony with them. Together with DNA, these structures form the network that carries light around the body.

The DNA carries the genetic code, and is a macro-molecule consisting of four chemical bases, arranged in pairs in a spiralling double chain — the *double helix*.

It has been found that when DNA absorbs light through one of its pairs, it is able to release this light later from another base pair, thus changing its frequency. This means that energy (the photon, see Figure 12) is passed from one base pair to another. Therefore, the bases can be regarded as effective light stores.

The absorption and storage of photons stimulate the attraction forces between molecules causing the DNA to contract. When there is a lack of photons outside the DNA molecule, the attraction forces inside the molecules decrease, causing the DNA to expand and light to be released.

It is assumed that these contractions and expansions happen rhythmically, due to rhythmic light effects on the organism, such as day and night or lunar phases, and that they therefore also form the basis for all biological rhythms.

Figure 13.

Conclusion

The precision and determination of processes within and between cells, and within the entire organism, have caused many scientists to talk of *in-built intelligence*. The appearance of co-operation and the way in which structures come together to form more complex structures, has inspired scientists to question whether there is a higher purpose working in nature.

The physical body of a tree is a living example of nature's impulse to work together; tens of thousands of leaves, miles of sap channels, myriads of cells — all united by a purpose.

The tree has a body filled with mainly sunlight. Light courses through its structure, navigating vital processes and maintaining the balance and health of the whole organism. Even the broadest and tallest tree can communicate a signal at the speed of light from one end of itself to the other. The tree produces a continuous light show from its very cells.

Figure 14. Kirlian photographs of an oak leaf and a yew twig.

Kirlian Photography

Kirlian Photography, named after the Soviet engineer, Semjon Kirlian, who developed it in 1939, reveals the distribution of charges upon the surface of objects. Generally, these charges appear as tiny lightning flashes, which seem to emerge from the object. In the case of living objects, such as the leaves of trees or human hands and feet, the charge distribution on the surface reflects the organism's internal movements of electricity and biophotons. Consequently, diagnostic conclusions about the health of that organism can be drawn from the photographs, as unhealthy plants will show different patterns of electricity and light from healthy plants.

5
Planets and Trees

Cosmic antennae

Radiation from supernova — the gigantic explosions marking the death of a star — has been shown to influence tree growth. In the mid 1970s scientists from the Botanical Institute of the Russian Academy of Sciences analysed the annual rings of a 807-year-old Juniper (*Juniperus turkistanicus*), which grew in the mountains of Tajikistan, on the upper tree line at the astonishing height of 3,500m (11,400 feet). Owing to the thin air the tree was exposed to more direct cosmic radiation than in lower areas.

After comparing the tree's annual rings with dates that supernova were known to have occurred — 1604, 1770 and 1952 — the scientists discovered that the tree's annual rings showed a definite slowing down of tree growth, sometimes even a virtual standstill, over the subsequent fifteen-year period. (Janik 1976, 1). The implication being that every star that dies in our galaxy is, therefore, perceived by trees.

The Moon and planets of the solar system influence life on Earth in other ways. A scientific method, known as the Drop Method, which determines the quality of water, has revealed the impact of planetary constellations on the formative forces of healthy water. Since all terrestrial life forms contain some amount of water, this technique suggests that all organisms are affected by cosmic events to a greater or lesser degree.

Figure 15. The 'drop technique' shows the formative forces active in water.
Top left: water from a clear mountain spring.
Top right: water from the same brook after exposure to pollutants.
Bottom row: water during a Jupiter-Neptune square. Left 12 minutes before; centre, at the time; right 12 minutes after.

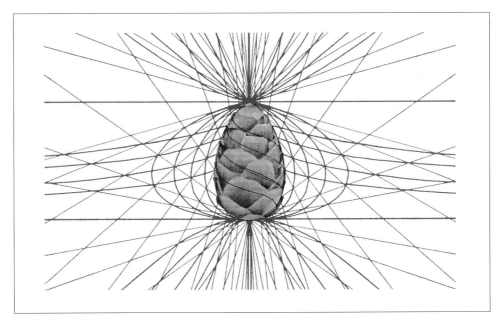

Figure 16. A triangle with one point in infinity has two parallel lines. Between them occurs a force field of path-curves. The harmonic proportions of the chosen numbers determine the character the forms will take. Here in the centre: the cone of Larch. (After Edwards).

Planetary rhythms and tree rhythms

During the course of his experiments on the leaf buds of deciduous trees the mathematician, Lawrence Edwards, made a discovery. During autumn and winter the leaf buds have a subtle pulsating movement. This is particularly astonishing since water or sap cannot be involved as, to avoid frost damage, the tree sheds its leaves and its metabolism stops during these seasons.

Over many winters, Edwards examined the leaf buds daily. After observing thousands and thousands of buds — mainly those of Oak, Beech, Ash, Elm, Birch and Cherry, as well as plants like Geranium, Primrose, Stitchwort and Knapweed — it became clear that they all possessed a fortnightly rhythm, which always occurred at the alignment of the Earth and Moon with a third celestial body. The identity of this third party was found to be specific for each plant species. Thus, Oak leaf buds expanded slightly at each Moon-Mars alignment (conjunctions and oppositions alike); Beech reacted to Moon-Saturn alignments; Elm was connected to

Mercury; Ash with the Sun; and Birch to Venus. The leaf buds of Cherry reacted at full moon and new moon, which was seen through minute contractions. These discoveries have all been measured and mathematically recorded (Edwards 1993).

Edwards found that, generally, the alignments stimulate a subtle expansion of the bud, but some species react in the opposite way and contract. For example, Oak and Geranium are both influenced by Mars, but while Oak buds expand at the times of relevant astronomical constellations, Geranium buds contract.

Without taking into account the fact that everything on Earth is a reflection of what is taking place in the cosmos, it is therefore impossible to understand plant life completely (Steiner 1993, 20).

It would be wrong, however, to expect every part of a plant to be a receptor for external influences. The natural rhythm of the plant is in permanent flux between reception and expression, contraction and expansion, inhalation and exhalation. Only the stages of contraction, such as leaf or flower buds, receive influences from cosmic forces. Stages of expansion, like leaves or flowers, are merely expressive of previously received patterns, rhythms, proportions and qualities.

Some interesting ideas about the influence of cosmic formative forces on plants are based on the work of Rudolf Steiner (see Bibliography). While most of the plant world sprouts, grows, blossoms and withers within the solar year, biannual plants reflect the stronger influence of Mars which also has a biannual cycle. Deciduous trees are particularly influenced by Jupiter's twelve-year cycle. As a result, trees can create structures that clearly last longer than the solar year on Earth. The

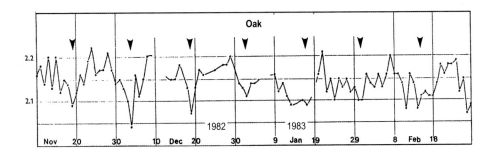

Figure 17. The pulsing of Oak leaf buds (measured in western Scotland, winter 1982–83). The numbers on the left represent the mean lambda value of the examined buds. A decrease in lambda resembles an expansion of the bud. The little arrows above the graph mark the Moon-Mars alignments. (After Edwards).

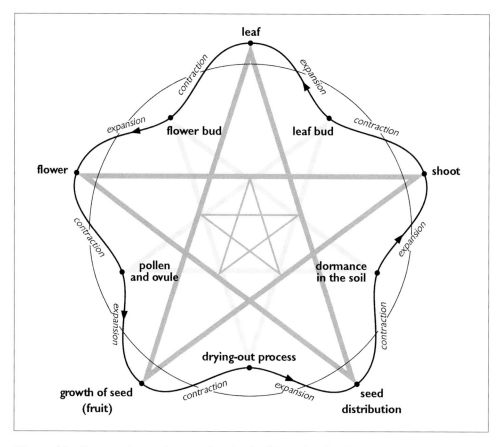

Figure 18. Contraction and expansion in the life cycle of a plant.

dominance of Jupiter, however, has yet another effect. Most trees in the temperate zone do not have colourful complicated blossoms, as reproduction in general is closely linked to the inner planets, particularly Venus and Mars. However, the far-reaching sphere of Jupiter does allow trees their wide, far-reaching shapes which expand abundantly into the surrounding space.

Shrubs fall between herbaceous plants and trees and have aspects of both. The influence of Jupiter allows them to grow for many years, and reach (compared to herbaceous plants) large sizes. On the other hand, the inner planets stimulate the more complex development of blossoms and fruit. This can easily be seen by comparing Rowan, Apple, Blackthorn and Hawthorn with Beech or Oak. The former group of trees have brighter flowers and juicy fruits, whereas the latter have modest blossoms and dry fruits.

Mars can cause an inhibition of growth, which often leads to spines or thorns, for example, Blackberry, Raspberry, Hawthorn and Blackthorn. Oak, which is strongly influenced by Mars, reflects the movements of this planet through the dominance of its branches and their bizarre zigzag growth, that changes direction all the time. The outline shape of the leaves also reveal the continuous rhythm of even phases of inhibition and contraction. This contractive principle is also manifest in tannic acid which has been used by humans for millennia to tan leather.

Since Mars' orbit is next to that of Earth, the distance between the two planets, as well as their movement in relation to each other, are constantly undergoing drastic changes. As a result, the influences of Mars alternate between phases of great and low intensity, and even phases of reversed direction.

With their annual foliating and shedding of leaves, the deciduous trees of the temperate zone are still rooted in the solar year, while most conifers of the temperate zone leave the limits of the solar year behind. They are evergreen and although they also have spring shoots, they keep growing until late autumn. In addition, their needles can last for about three years on Pine, and more than six years on Spruce. Many of the world's oldest trees are conifers; for example, Redwoods and Yew. The ripening of conifer fruits is also not necessarily confined to the solar year; thus, the Juniper seeds take two years to ripen. Of course, there are exceptions; Larch sheds its needles every autumn, and Alder, which is a leafy tree, takes two years for its cones to ripen. The forces which inhibit growth processes, contract substance and harden the forms of conifers, originate from Saturn (see Spruce, page 201).

These accounts suggest that one should not jump to conclusions. Although Beech reacts to the movements of Saturn it is not a *Saturn tree,* unlike Spruce, which you can tell at a glance. The soft bends of Beech's branches, with their bright, downy leaves, and readiness to reach out far into the space around it, reveal Jupiter as the dominant force in leafy trees, such as Beech.

Trees, like the whole of vegetation, breathe and pulse in rhythms of cyclic time. During the autumn they draw their essence inwards and compress it in processes which produce seeds. The leaf buds on the twigs wait all winter for the big day in spring when they, together with the seeds below, open up to the light and the air of their surroundings (Edwards 1993, 256).

During the four or five weeks after the winter solstice, the pulsing of plant buds becomes even smaller; the Earth has *inhaled* fully and is waiting. Finally, in the spring, all vessels burst open and unfold. The Earth *exhales* until the full splendour of the summer solstice. Thus, the natural world moves rhythmically, and the movements of the stars are reflected in the ground beneath our feet.

More about rhythms

The intervals in which the buds pulse all have a frequency of about two weeks owing to the Moon which revolves around the Earth approximately every twenty-eight days. Twice a month it therefore crosses the imaginary axis of Earth and any other planet aligned with it. Planetary conjunctions and oppositions occur at slightly different intervals. However, the mean frequencies are 14.77 days for the Moon aligning with the Sun, Mercury or Venus; 14.23 days for the Moon's alignment with Mars; 13.75 days for the alignment of the Moon and Jupiter; and 13.7 days for the Moon and Saturn's alignment.

Planets affect each other's influences. The swelling of Beech leaf buds (usually stimulated by Saturn), is considerably smaller during a Mars-Saturn conjunction. Conjunctions of Saturn with Jupiter have a similar effect. This interaction occurs when any planet comes within five or six degrees of the specific planet related to a particular plant species.

Lawrence Edwards also discovered a Beech tree that did not react with the constellations. Looking for reasons he noticed a transformer station not far from the tree. A sign on the door read: "Danger — 30,000 Volts!" Subsequent examinations of other plants below high-power lines have proved that artificial electromagnetic fields cut the plants off almost completely from interstellar rhythms.

Over the years another phenomenon has been identified — the *phase-shift*. Although each species has its own rhythm, nature also seems to pre-empt astronomical aspects, For example, a plant reaction that coincided with a planetary alignment in the first year, happens about a day before the same constellation in the following year, and about two days earlier in the third year. This process continues until after about seven years the zero point is reached again, and after staying at this point for a little while, the next phase-shift then begins.

No cosmic cycle has been identified that might stimulate this seven-year rhythm, but human beings are also influenced by a seven-year rhythm — it takes the human body seven years to replace all its cells. The science of Anthroposophy counts the phases of man's inner development in groups of seven years, and most cultures have divided time into weeks of seven days.

We begin to see this world in which we live as a vast organism, in which the roles of planet and plant are intimately interwoven, one with the other. No star can move, but a plant responds. (Edwards 1993, 255)

6
Forests through the Ages

Early agriculture

Early agricultural settlers in Neolithic Europe found the land thickly covered with dense wildwood. Every livelihood, village or field had to be carved out of the primeval vegetation. Agriculture spread over this continent through a method called *slash and burn.* This *burning*-economy, which is still seen today in the tropical rain forests, provided virgin soil with an ash dressing, ready for farming.

With the coming of the Iron Age Celts, who used iron tools and heavy ploughs, the tilling of clay soils became possible and whole new areas were converted to cultivated land.

These events took place over vast stretches of time. Subsequent generations changed the face of the Earth very slowly, until the first large-scale ecological crises appeared in Classical times in the Mediterranean, and during the Middle Ages, north of the Alps when human over-population destroyed the last European wildwoods.

However, because these changes happened so slowly they were completely invisible to the individual or social group at any given time before the Middle Ages. The ancients of Europe only saw the circular rebirth of nature in the course of the seasons of the year.

They did not take anything for granted, and still felt the connection with nature, giving thanks to the Great Goddess, the omnipresent and omnipotent Earth Mother. They praised the Moon for her gifts of fertility, and celebrated with the Sun's annual journey of ascent and descent, death and rebirth. They prayed to the Corn-Mother and revered the Horned One, the mighty Lord of the Forest. They made their peace with the spirits of the animals before the hunt. They were not afraid of death for they understood life in its cyclic movement.

However, some early civilizations did not confine their numbers; they overpopulated, and had no means of grasping the ecological consequences which they caused.

Anno domini

Naturally, people always lived off the land. They depended on it and exploited it, but they also respected and cared for it. Sages and priests of indigenous cultures used to remind their peoples that man is a part of the whole, that man belongs to Earth and not Earth to man.

The Romans exploited their colonies, leaving ecological disasters and mental and social chaos everywhere. Tribal bonds and links with the land were broken. People learned from their oppressors how to calculate for their own advantage and have an eye for wealth, power and prestige. Druidism, which had maintained a sense of natural balance, was annihilated as an influential social force as greed took over. The Dark Ages began.

In the centuries that followed, Christianity was a comfort to many, but it too desecrated the land and put forward an increasingly materialistic view that eventually turned woodlands into products, and sanctuaries into factories.

The Christian 'crusade' against trees, particularly sacred trees, is unparalleled in history. Previously, sacred groves had sometimes been damaged or destroyed only during periods of warfare. In fourth-century Gaul, Martin, Bishop of Tours, started the sad tradition of destroying sacred groves for *religious* reasons. In the second half of the seventh century AD, the five sacred trees of Ireland were destroyed. In AD 723, at a sanctuary belonging to tribes of German Saxons in Geismar (central Germany), St Boniface not only felled the Sacred Oak of Donar (also known as Thor), but also poisoned the sacred spring. In AD 772, according to entries in the Frankish annals, during his conquest of the Saxons, Charles the Great destroyed the Irmin-pillar in Westphalia, Germany, which was the major Saxon sanctuary at the time.

As late as the beginning of the eleventh century, the Frisians and Saxons still venerated sacred groves in the remoter parts of the diocese of Bishop Unwan of Bremen. He therefore ordered all such woods to be cut down. Further to the east, in 1093, Bretislav, Prince of Bohemia, burnt down the heathen groves and trees in his land. In 1386, Yagello, the Grand Duke of Lithuania, adopted Christianity as the national religion and felled the sacred groves of his country. His subjects however, chose remote places in the depths of the Lithuanian woodlands, where *heathen* rites and festivals continued for centuries.

However, the biggest impact of the Church is that in the fourteenth century, wood finally emerged as a marketable resource — a product with a price.

Deforestation and replanting

It is a well-documented fact that the wealth of the Middle Ages came from the forest. Fast-growing populations, increased farming, wooden architecture, city fires, fuel-consuming industries such as metal, salt and glass production, and later boat-building, all depleted the European forests. Central Europe would have become desert if the climate had not been ideal for rapid reforestation.

In AD 1368, a councillor in Nuremberg, Bavaria, planted fast-growing Norway Spruce, Silver Fir and Pine trees and saved the economy of his hometown in the long run. It was quite a revolutionary act to discover the potential of conifers as the raw material of the future, while the Middle Ages had viewed them as worthless trees.

By the eighteenth century, the depletion of the central European woodlands had resulted in vast areas of barren wasteland. Foresters, pressured by demands for profitable timber production — for wood was still the most important building material and fuel — were left with the task of reforesting the wastelands. For these reasons, and because of the ecological situation in the eroded wastelands, reforestation was only possible with the robust Norway Spruce and Pine. This practice established the dominance of conifers in many forests that can still be observed today.

The effects of the early industrial age would have been far more devastating for European forests if it had not been for the large amounts of wood imported from colonies in America and Africa. When the New World was discovered, nearly half of the North American continent was covered with wildwood.

> Forests of giant maple, chestnut and oak stretched from the east
> coast to the Mississippi valley. Spruce and pine carpeted the
> Great Lakes region. Ancient redwood and Douglas fir towered
> over the Pacific Ocean.
> 　　　　　(http://www.saveamericasforests.org, June 2000)

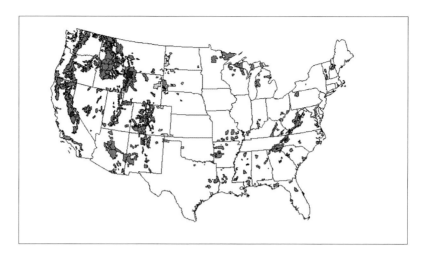

Figure 19. Wildwood destruction in the United States. From Save America's Forests website.

These forests along the Pacific coast are the largest non-tropical rain forests on Earth. Former American president, Theodore Roosevelt, has been quoted as saying:

> A grove of giant Redwoods and Sequoias should be maintained in the same way as a great and beautiful cathedral. (Struss 1986)

If only he had said 'will be kept.' The coastal Redwood lands were sold for a price of $2.50 an acre to private companies that carried out huge legalized clear felling operations. Today, only about five per cent of primeval woodland is left. In 1999, a 35 m (120 feet), mature Red Cedar was worth up to $2,200 at the mill. The chainsaws are still roaring, but against growing resistance. In 1997, Senator Robert Torricelli introduced the Act to Save America's Forests in both Houses of the American Congress.

> The Act will end clear cutting on all federal lands and stop logging and road building in the last wild, road-less and ancient forests. (http://www.saveamericasforests.org, June 2000)

Monocultures — the beginning of the end

Who has not seen the dark, uniform forests in which Spruce trees stand strictly to attention like soldiers, in line after line? The governments of European countries recommend these forests for recreation, but are they forest? Most European countries do not have much, if any, true primeval forest left. The majority is not wildwood but *monoculture*. Pure stands of Spruce or Pine on poor soil are susceptible to infection and storm damage. In Great Britain only eleven per cent of the total land area is covered with woodland, and most of this is made up of conifer plantations. Only one fifteenth of this area is semi-natural native woodland, and is managed for conservation purposes. Following heavy storm damage at the beginning of the century, a German forester stated:

> *Willst du den Wald vernichten, so pflanze nichts als Fichten!*
> If you want to destroy the forest, plant nothing but spruce.

Viktor Schauberger also criticized modern forestry techniques. He said that at one time young saplings lived for decades in healthy, naturally-growing forest, uninfluenced by man and his technology, and protected by the mother tree. and responding to the balance of temperature, humidity and light. With the destruction of the mother trees, the saplings reached out to enjoy direct warmth and light (Alexandersson 1990).

Young trees are particularly sensitive to direct light and heat. Only later, when the previous generation fades, are they ready to use a surplus of direct light and warmth for their own reproduction. When exposed to too much sun, young trees develop artificial extra-growth, which results in unusually broad annual rings, and soft wood of inferior quality. The tree tries to protect itself with side shoots, to shade and cool the trunk, and the wood is further devalued by many knots. It also dries irregularly and cracks easily.

Modern forestry, however, cares more for quantity than quality. The mother trees are felled, *rejuvenating* the wood, to stimulate this artificial growth. When young trees started to shade each other and their metabolism was able to relax, the woodland thinned out again.

Varieties of undergrowth are the first to disappear with the old trees, followed by the wildlife, both vegetable and animal. The complexity of the forest ecosystem vanishes and is replaced by a man-controlled, uniform monoculture.

In natural mixed forest, certain trees and shrubs can take direct light, and shield other life forms in the wood. Protected from the Sun, strong winds and heavy rains, the younger plants can grow inside the forest. They can take their time to mature and their seeds are of outstanding quality.

However, in a pure stand there is an imbalance. One kind of root system exhausts only one layer of ground. All the trees have to fight for the same water, the same nutrients and the same light frequencies. More light energy is reflected than in a mixed forest; this causes a temperature rise, which adversely affects the already overheated trees.

Trees like water have a natural urge to cool themselves; like humans, they are sensitive to internal temperature changes. With the slightest rise in temperature a person starts to feel ill. The human body fights viruses and bacteria by raising the temperature further. However, a tree cannot produce fever. Instead, it attracts the growth of certain fungi, which ultimately kill the tree. Bark beetles and some other parasites are the 'health police of nature' (Schauberger) — they are the effect of ill trees not the cause.

New symptoms of tree damage

In industrial parts of Europe and North America, the introduction of high smokestacks, that distribute poisons more evenly over wider areas, paralleled an increase in various symptoms of tree damage and the mass dying of trees. Industrial nations finally had to admit that the pollution of the biosphere could not continue at the same rate.

Since the 1950s our biosphere has not only been poisoned by chemical pollution, but has also been bombarded by man-made radioactive emissions, electro-stress, and an increasing amount of microwaves released from television, radio and mobile phone transmitters. All these factors interact in various ways, making our environment ever more hostile. Trees rarely die from one thing, but from an overwhelming variety of assaults on their health.

The dramatic ups and downs in the history of tree cover reveal that we have challenged nature more than once, causing apocalyptic scenarios — wastelands, deserts, floods, avalanches and hurricanes. Yet there were periods when man and nature worked together. Despite the internal over-exploitation of trees, two hundred years later, a third of Germany is again covered with trees. In Britain, tree cover has now risen to eleven per cent from its lowest point of four per cent after World War II.

After caring for quantity, the time has now come to work for quality. This means loosening up the straight lines of monoculture, mixing conifers with broadleaf trees, allowing more mixed woodlands in general, and defining areas were nature can be left to itself to eventually create new virgin forests for centuries to come.

7

The Sacred Grove

Trees have played a significant role, both physically and spiritually,in the development of human life.

In the very beginning, hominids lived in the shelter of the woods, just as apes still do today. When we left the woods for the open savannahs, we discovered fire and its use (see Chapter 1). Fire became the driving force in the development of the human species, as it rose to dominance in whatever habitat; it was always trees which supported the human need for fuel.

When early humans started to actively change their environment by building shelters, huts, houses, bridges, fences and barns, wood was again of vital importance. Most of the stone tools from the Stone Age served to work wood, and this lasted until the building of the great medieval cities which were built — and often re-built — mostly in wood.

Owing to their dependency on wood, the early settlements soon designated certain parts of the woodland for growing sustainable wood supplies (Rackham 1980, 48). In general, they were known as *coppices*. In a coppice trees were cut every four to ten years just above their root or stump. Some species react very well to the stimulated growth that ensues. The life span of Hazel trees is even increased under such conditions.

Other parts of the woodland, identified by elders, seers, shamans or priests, were consecrated. Mainly left to themselves, the sacred groves were only visited for spiritual reasons, such as prayer, meditation or thanksgiving. Classical sources describe how a Greek warrior, out of gratitude for his success in battle, would hang his best weapons onto a sacred tree. They would then stay there until they fell apart, alongside other offerings like animal skins and horns, tools from craftsmen or jewellery offered by rich people. For most of history, until only very recently, humans not only took from nature, but also attempted to give back as well.

Sacred groves

The Greeks and Romans

Almost everywhere in the world the beginnings of social and religious life took place under trees. On all continents humans chose the presence of special trees for this kind of activity. The first places of worship were usually simple altars placed under such trees which were often decorated with a wealth of offerings. Much later, the altars were surrounded by small temples. Even the huge temple complexes of early history, such as the Acropolis, kept their attached sacred trees or groves. The religious life of Classical Greece can be better characterized by sacred groves than by white marble temples. Each Greek deity was linked with a particular tree species

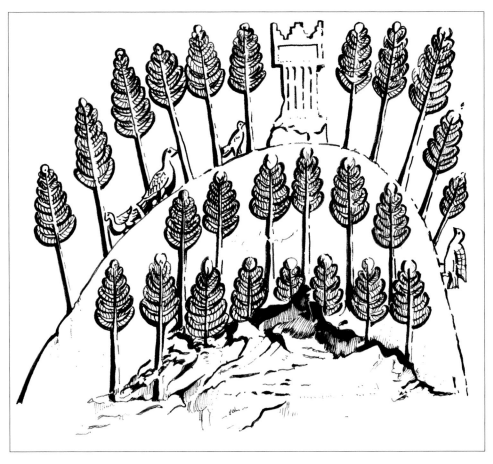

Figure 20. Sacred grove with temple, palace relief from Dur-Sharrukin, Assyria, c. 700 BC. (After Yarden).

and worshipped under it — for example, the Laurel was consecrated to Apollo, the Myrtle-tree to Aphrodite, the Olive to Athena, and the Pine tree to Pan.

What we today label as *gods* were originally the spirits of trees to whom goodwill and gratitude was bestowed. This is not at all surprising when we remember that Athens owed its economical power to the olive trade, as did Lebanon to the Cedar-of-Lebanon, and Phoenicia to the Phoenix or Date palm *(Phoenix dactylifera)* after which it was named. The figure of Zeus developed from the dryad of the prophetic oak in the Sacred Grove of Dodona, a pilgrimage destination for about two thousand years, until the fourth century AD (Graves 1975, 1.33). As an oracle, it was as famous as that of Delphi which was originally an Apollo-Laurel sanctuary. Everywhere in ancient Greece the politically or judicially persecuted could find asylum in sacred groves, a concept that was taken up much later by the Christian Church (Philpot 1994, 49).

The Romans adopted many things from the Greeks, and with the deities they imported the consecration of the corresponding tree species. Countless sacred groves were situated on the Seven Hills of Rome. In one of them, King Numa was believed to have received the Laws of Rome from the Oak dryad, Egeria. The Fig tree was also honoured as the founding tree of Rome because it had given shelter to the She-wolf which suckled Romulus and Remus.

Celts and Druids

Further to the north and west, the Celtic and Germanic tribes never built temples around the altars in their sacred groves. Shamans work mainly with *life forces*, and what other environment could have been more suitable for that, than a grove, in the heart of a wood where fertility and vitality are almost tangible? The Druids also used stone circles which they inherited from pre-Celtic Neolithic cultures, but the centres of their activities were the groves. The word *Druid* stems from Sanskrit *dru* (tree, wood) and *wid, vid* (knowledge, seeing), an Indo-European derivative. Druid therefore denotes one with tree or wood knowledge. The training for Druids took about twenty years, most of it in remote places in the woodlands, and their association of trees with knowledge and understanding can be seen in the Ogham alphabet— the Druidic alphabet in which each letter bears the name of a tree.

Early alphabets were not only used to store or transmit information but also for divination and magic. Originally, alphabets were powerful sets of ideas and concepts, denoting the principal forces of life. It can be argued that the invention of alphabets brought more potent changes for human societies than that of agriculture. In many cultures the skills of reading and writing, as well as learning and enlightenment in general, were strongly associated with trees. In ancient Egypt, Djahuti (Thoth), the god of scripture, and Seshat, a goddess associated with the Tree of Knowledge, would write a pharaoh's name on to the leaves of the Egyptian World Tree, thereby ensuring that he would live forever. In Norse myth, the sky god, Odin, hung himself upside down from the World Tree for nine days and nights, to gain divine knowledge. On his return, he brought his people the runes — a set of concepts and letters similar to the Celtic Ogham. The first European books were written on beech wood tablets, hence the similarities in many languages for the words for both book and beech; for example, in German *Buch* and *Buche*; in Swedish, *bok* and *bok*, and so on.

Trees were so significant in people's lives that many Celtic tribes named themselves after trees; for example, the Eurobones and Eburovices of Gaul, named after the Gaulish word *eburos*, the Yew tree, as was the Irish tribe, the Iverni. Other examples are the Gaulish Lemnovices, (the People of the Elm), and the Arverni, (the People from the Land of the Alder).

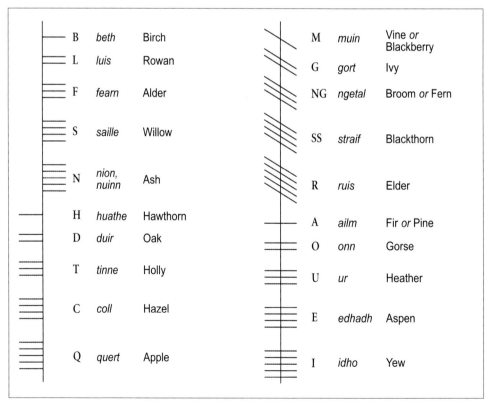

Figure 21. The Old Irish ogham alphabet

Figure 22. Reconstruction of the wooden circle at Sarn y Bryn Caled, Wales, c.2000 BC. (After Gibson 1998).

The Anglo-Saxon and Norse tribes meanwhile met for council, jurisdiction, annual festivals and all important gatherings under their sacred trees, particularly Yew and Lime (Linden). Tacitus reported in the first century AD that the ancient Germans took great care to bury the dead with the wood of particular trees *(Germania, 27)*. Trees were guardians, in both life and death.

However, the use of special woods in social and religious contexts goes much further back in time than the Iron and Bronze Ages. When the first standing stones were erected at Stonehenge about 2550 BC they replaced a much older wooden circle. In fact, many other stone circles in Wales and Scotland had a wooden origin. During their periods of use, both Stonehenge and Avebury were accompanied by circles of wooden posts for ritual use. Under the present car park at Stonehenge the remains of a wooden circle have been discovered which is between three and four thousand years older than Stonehenge. Today, we cannot know exactly which activities took place in the sacred groves, and which ones occurred in and around the circles of wooden posts, but it is likely that major festivals were held in open spaces around the ceremonial centre of the wooden circle, rather than taking place in the sacred grove.

Biblical tradition

In Jewish tradition, trees have also been of great significance. When the Israelites reached the Promised Land they adopted the tradition of worshipping God at tree sanctuaries called *ashêra*, from the preceding Canaanites. The Lord first appeared to Moses in the vision of the Burning Bush, and in his final words before his death, Moses referred to the Lord as '... him that dwelt in the bush.' (Deut. 33:16). Moses' staff was cut from an Almond tree *(Amygdalus communis)*, the most sacred tree in ancient Israel; its ancient Semitic name, amygdala, meaning 'Great Mother.' After his death, Moses' staff was handed down from generation to generation as the sceptre of the kings of Israel, which is mirrored by the staff of the Pope.

Moses crafted the Ark of the Covenant, in which he placed the Ten Commandments, from wood of the sacred Acacia *(Acacia arabica)*, which in Egypt, where he had lived a long time, was the tree consecrated to Osiris, the spirit of vegetation who was resurrected annually.

Abraham settled near the Grove of Mamre, a sacred grove of Terebinth or Turpentine trees *(Pistacia terebinthus)*, where the Lord appeared to him (Gen. 18:1), and where he later wanted to be buried. Deborah, the mother of Israel, was buried beneath the sacred Oak of Beth-El, which was also a Terebinth (Gen. 35:8; 35:19). In the legendary temple of King Solomon (tenth century BC) the only and re-occuring motif in the wall decorations of the inner and outer shrines was the Tree of Life (see Hageneder, *The Heritage of Trees*).

Jesus of Nazareth might have challenged the patriarchal establishment of his time, but he acted in harmony with a time-honoured tradition when he taught his disciples, 'as usual,' in the sacred Olive grove of Gethsemane (Luke 22:39). For his last night on Earth he went there again — '... Jesus often met there with his disciples' (John 18:2) — and in fear of the coming day of torture and death he went to the trees on his own and 'there appeared to him an angel from heaven bringing him strength' (Luke 22:43).

In Eastern Europe, Slav and Baltic peoples also sought strength in their sacred groves, and even in the seventeenth, eighteenth and nineteenth centuries Christian missionaries were trying to stop them from doing so. In remote villages of India one can still find holy trees.

The World Tree

Why are trees everywhere in the world intimately connected with learning and spiritual growth? How did the sages of the past perceive the tree, thus giving it such a central role in their understanding of the world? Archaeology and mythology have uncovered a great deal of evidence which partly answers these questions, and the resulting picture is remarkably unified, international and pan-religious.

First of all, the World Tree represents the whole universe. Everything that exists is part of the World or Cosmic Tree. It is rooted in the primeval beginning and its abundant crown carries created life forms. The Tree is not merely a symbol of the universe — the underlying, invisible structure of existence has the shape of a tree, which is animated by the spirit of God. Since the all-encompassing World Tree is imbued with divine spirit everything, including the tree shape, was therefore believed to be sacred. However, in many places trees were especially revered for being pure manifestations of the spirit of creation.

In the physical world, the archetypal pattern of the spiritual tree appears time and time again, in plants as well as in the branching forms of the blood and nervous systems of animals and humans. Even the network of nerves in the human brain, located on top of the spine (*trunk*), resembles the Cosmic Tree — 'As above, so below' (*The Emerald Tablet*). This idea can also be found in ancient scriptures of Egyptian, Hebrew and Sanskrit origin (Yarden 1971, 41). Ancient yoga teachings of India have Kundalini energy dormant at the *root* of the spine, and try to awaken it to rise to the *crown* (note the tree language).

The tree shape is an inherent structure not only in the physical world. The psychologist, Carl Gustav Jung, likened the human psyche to a tree: it has roots in the dark world of the subconscious, and through the work of the conscious mind (trunk) the true individuality (crown) can unfold. In Buddhism, this process of self-realization is called *enlightenment*. The sacred Pippala tree *(Ficus religiosa)* helped Buddha to achieve the ultimate and unconditioned truth *(bodhi)* and was therefore called the Bodhi Tree — the Tree of Enlightenment. By growing beyond himself, Buddha became one with the Cosmic Tree, the whole universe. This is why, in early Buddhism, Buddha was not depicted in human form, but as a tree. The Bodhi Tree — and not Buddha — was called *the Great Awakener.*

The Tree of Life

The Cosmic Tree usually stands in a protected enclosure, or paradisical garden, and in many sources is guarded by a snake or dragon, which represents the spirit of the Earth guarding the gift of life. Since the World Tree contains all life, it nourishes all life, and its seeds contain all plant and animal species. It is therefore also the Tree of Life. It is self-healing, all-healing and immortal. It gives freely to all creatures, even its immortality, either by means of its sacred fruits (the apples of the Hesperides in Greek myth, the apples of immortality in Norse myth) or by its sap.

This precious liquid was called *soma* in ancient India and *haoma* in ancient Persia, while among Celtic, Saxon and Norse tribes it was known as the liquid from the 'sacred cauldron' of inspiration. The Hindu *Vedas* praise it for 'generating hymns with the powers of a poet.' The Welsh Bardic tradition called it the 'mead of the poets,' and in Norse tradition it was 'the exciter of spirit.' In sixth century BC Persia the king and high priest, Zoroaster,

Figure 23. In the afterworld, the soul of the dead bows down and receives the Water of Life from the tree goddess, who also offers food. Hieroglyphic funeral papyrus of the Royal Scribe and Chief Military Officer, Nakht, c. 1350–1300 BC. (After Cook 1992).

saw the Tree of Life as giving 'strength and health to the body, and to the soul enlightenment and eternal life' (Philpot 1994, 123). In Egypt, too, the land was full of trees supplying food for the living — figs, dates, almonds — and the realm of the dead was full of trees bestowing the food and drink of the soul.

The earliest Indian scriptures, the *Vedas* and *Upanishads* (c. 900–500 BC) emphasize the spiritual origin of the World Tree. In the creation myth, the creative god, Brahma, is a tree who bears all other deities as his branches.

> This universe is a tree eternally existing, its root aloft, its branches
> spread below. The pure root of the tree is Brahman, the immortal ...
> who is verily the Self. (*Katha Upanishad, VI,* 1)

The notion that the World Tree grows upside down, from the world of spirit down into the realm of physical manifestations, can also be found in the *Kabbalah,* the ancient mystical lore of Judaism. The Kabbalistic Tree of Life holds the knowledge of how the adept can grow beyond personal limitations and unite with the divine source.

The Tree of Light and the Tree of Knowledge

Since ancient times, and in many nations — particularly Egypt, Mesopotamia and Greece — the celestial bodies were seen as fruits of the World Tree. A natural aspect of the Tree of Life is therefore the Tree of Light. In Jewish tradition, it developed into the Menorah, the seven-branched candleholder, which represents the aspects of divine light shining into the world. In ancient Mesopotamia, where astronomy and astrology were developed, these seven elements were called Sun, Moon, Mercury, Venus, Mars, Jupiter and Saturn.

Since the Tree of Life bestows all nourishment this also includes food for the heart and spirit. It is also the Tree of Knowledge. This was regarded as a positive thing by everyone except the Christian Church, which split the Tree into two; the half which was called the *Tree of Knowledge of Good and Evil* became taboo. Elsewhere it remained one tree, and even in the Bible its original unity can still be glimpsed in places (Gen 2:9). For example, Eve says to the serpent: 'We may eat of the fruit of the trees of the garden; but God said, "You shall not eat of the fruit of *the tree* which is in the midst of the garden".' (Gen 3:2f). Later, after Adam and Eve are expelled from Eden, the Lord sends cherubim 'to guard the way to the tree of life' (Gen 3:24).

In ancient India, the leaves of the World Tree were called *Veda* (knowledge), since wisdom and understanding facilitate spiritual growth. The World Tree is at one with everything, and a mystical union with it therefore also brings knowledge. This is why Siberian shamans *climbed* the World Tree to reach the spirit worlds; why Druids were taught the secrets of the woods

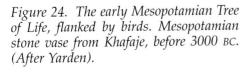

Figure 24. The early Mesopotamian Tree of Life, flanked by birds. Mesopotamian stone vase from Khafaje, before 3000 BC. (After Yarden).

Figure 25. The Menorah, the Tree of Light, developed from the seven-branched Tree of Life. (After Yarden).

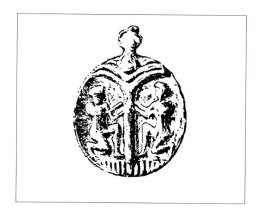

Figure 26. Praying couple at the Tree, golden amulet from Susa, fourth millennium BC *(pre-Persian).*

in sacred groves; how Odin, descending from his tree, was able to bring back the runes to his people; how Buddha returned from the tree sanctuary with the understanding of the ultimate liberation; and why peoples all over the world have meditated and prayed beneath trees. Zoroaster said: 'To the soul it [the Tree] is the way to heaven.' (Philpot 1994, 123).

Christian Europe

The early patriarchs of the Roman Church knew about and respected these ancient traditions. Hippolytos, the third century presbyter of Rome, praised the Tree of Life in his Easter speech as 'the firm basis of the universe, the calm centre of all things, the foundation of the world's circle, the cosmic hinge.' However, a century later, the systematic destruction of sacred groves began. The Tree of Life was twisted into the *Tree of Temptation,* almost as evil as the satanic serpent that tempted Eve. During the next sixteen centuries this interpretation clouded the European relationship with all of nature.

Nevertheless, some old customs survived throughout the Christian period, such as the Yule log, the Life Rod, and the maypole. The maypole or tree was usually a young Birch that was brought into the village, festively decorated, and made the central point of celebrations for the return of summer. The Yule log, a piece of wood from a special tree, was ceremonially burned on New Year's Eve and some of its ashes scattered on to the fields as a blessing, while the rest were kept in the house as a talisman. The Life Rod was a branch of an extremely vital tree — usually Rowan, Willow, Hazel or Juniper — which was used to symbolically beat the cattle, sheep and, in some places, children, to bestow nature's regenerative powers, health and fertility upon them.

Another ancient custom — a festively decorated tree for mid-winter celebrations — disappeared until its rediscovery in late eighteenth century Germany. Within a few decades the Christmas tree spread like wildfire all over the Western world.

Into the twenty-first century

What can mankind learn from the distant and recent past to transform the Earth back into the paradise it was meant to be?

Mankind can plant, tend and protect trees, since the deforested planet needs trees to maintain the benevolent conditions of the biosphere. However, it is also important to re-awaken the respect for life within human society and ourselves. When this is present all threatened life forms, including our own species, can only benefit.

Some decades ago, the indigenous people of America taught us that everything has a spirit. The next part of this book looks at different tree species, with regard to their unique qualities and characters, and reveals how each tree embodies different aspects of the *spirit* of the Tree of Life.

PART II

THE ESSENCE OF TREES

In the eyes of a seer, every leaf of a tree is a page in the Holy Book and contains divine revelation ...

Hazrat Inayat Khan

Let me cut no tree without holy need. Let me not tread into a flowering field. Let me always plant trees. The gods look with goodwill upon those who plant trees along roads, at home, holy places, crossroads and houses.

When you marry, plant a wedding tree. When a child is born, plant a tree. When a loved one dies, plant a tree for his or her soul.

At all festivals, for all-important occasions, visit trees. Prayers are hallowed by trees.

From a Lithuanian prayer

Observation

The following selection of tree species is neither in alphabetical order nor does it attempt to follow botanical classification. Instead, its structure is directed by the tree traditions of Europe, the myths, legends, folklore, customs and history. The selection includes the trees of the ancient Irish ogham (see Chapter 7), interspersed with other trees which, after the last Ice Age, spread over northwest Europe of their own accord. Smaller shrubs and trees — namely Elder, Blackthorn, Hazel, Hawthorn, Holly, Juniper and even Ivy (not a tree at all) — are included because of their strong presence in the hearts and minds of peoples; a presence is disproportionate to their physical size. The Horse Chestnut, on the other hand, is not included, because it only survived the Ice Age in a small and remote valley of Eastern Europe where it remained until its discovery in 1576. Consequently, it does not feature at all in Celtic, Anglo-Saxon or Greek tradition. In a similar way, the Sycamore, unlike the related Field Maple, does not hold a big place in European legend and folklore because, for the greater part of history, it was confined to areas around the Alps.

For reasons of space and the abundance of material, other *genera* of the temperate zone, such as Walnut, Hickory, Olive and Cypress, as well as a number of American trees, have had to be excluded.

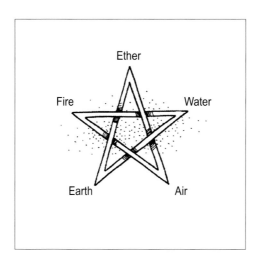

Figure 27.
The alchemical
pentangle.

Owing to the nature of the anthropological material the chapter about Spruce also deals with Fir. The loyalty to botanical terminology has been sacrificed at certain points to promote a more direct understanding of the historical material and its spiritual meaning.

The composition of the single portraits is loosely based on the alchemical pentangle which has the five classical elements attached to its points (Figure 27).

EARTH stands for the physical appearance of the tree, its biology, metabolism and behaviour in time (the seasons) and space (soil preferences and general distribution). These sections are written by my old friend, Martin Klatt, a German painter who has spent a great deal of time living with trees.

WATER denotes the waters of healing. Food and remedies have always been provided by trees. Recipes just containing apples or hazelnuts could fill a whole bookshelf, and there are many others: spring salads with birch or lime leaves, rowan jelly, elderflower wine, and many more. Cures, antiseptics and first-aid remedies are also numerous. For reasons of space, only a few, typical examples are cited for each tree. Another reason for keeping this section short is that I do not want to inadvertently encourage readers to drill the last healthy birches for their sap, dig out alder roots, or strip the bark off poplars and oaks. There are simply not enough trees. I do include some recipes, however, for those who wish to absorb something of a tree on a physical level. These do not involve the mass exploitation of our remaining trees. The use of tree essences in classical homeopathy, and in Bach Flower remedies, is also included.

Until recently, not many trees have been part of the traditional list of homeopathic remedies. However, over the past three or four years, interest has grown considerably in homeopathic remedies from trees, particularly native ones. The results of a large international project on the testing of homeopathic remedies have only recently appeared in the journal *Homeopathic Links*. At the moment clinical trials are continuing, but many correlations have already been made between certain trees and specific conditions.

AIR is the medium for the sung and spoken word, as paper and stone carry the written one. These three media have carried, and the latter two preserved, part of our ancestors' tree knowledge. Most myths, legends and customs referred to in this section were originally passed on orally.

FIRE is the element closest to spirit, and transforms the other three, burning particularly in air (oxygen). This section tries to conjure up the spiritual element of the other three sections, particularly those of the oral traditions (Air), thus revealing a glimpse of the eternal spirit of the tree.

ETHER, the fifth element, was traditionally the bridge, or channel, between primal creative forces and their elemental manifestations. It is represented here by a painting dedicated to the tree. Poetry and art speak to the soul and heart, whereas photography alone binds us to our habitual ways of visual perception.

Botanical Basics

All trees have a basic structure consisting of a root system, trunk and crown. The roots collect food and anchor the trunk, which supports the crown and raises it towards the light. Trunk and branches give the tree its visible shape. While a big part of the wood and bark consists of dead cells, the living parts of the tree are the cambium, leaves, sap channels that connect the roots with the buds, leaves, flowers and fruits.

The roots

The roots are long underground *branches* that provide anchorage for the tree and absorb water containing dissolved minerals from the soil. In most cases roots are attracted initially towards the centre of the Earth (geotropism); the first movement of a germinating seed is downwards. In young roots a thick cortex protects a central cylinder consisting of the *vascular tissue* — the xylem and the phloem channels. In secondary root growth, parenchyma cells between the xylem and phloem become cambium cells which create new (secondary) xylem and phloem. Eventually, the cambium tissue forms a cylinder similar to that in the trunk and branches. Larger roots do not absorb moisture as their bark is quite impervious to liquid.

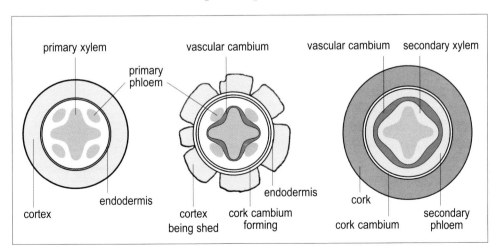

Figure 28. Secondary root growth.
Left: Young root.   Centre: Beginning of secondary growth.   Right: Mature root.

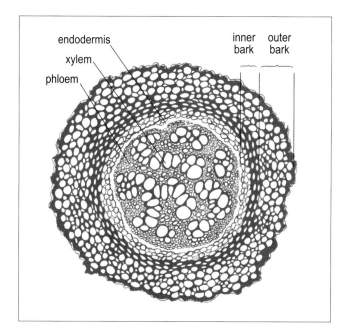

Figure 29. Cross-section of a young pine root, magnified 60 times. (After Bracegirdle & Miles, 1971.)

A tree develops countless smaller roots. Every spring each root grows longer at its tip, which pushes through the particles of soil. Thousands of fine root hairs grow just behind the root tip, which increase the contact surface of root and soil for the more effective absorption of water and nutrients. Water passes through the cortex of the root, moving through the living cells of the endodermis, which controls the water intake to the roots. Once inside the vascular cylinder the water meets the xylem, which carries the sap to the crown and distributes it to every leaf and fruit.

Many forest trees co-operate with special kinds of fungi in the soil. Fungi are unable to photosynthesize, and trees supply them with carbohydrates

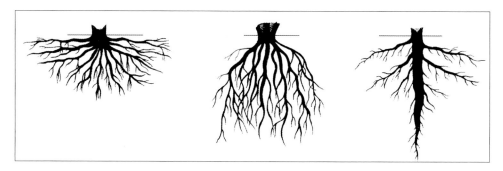

Figure 30. Different types of root systems. Most trees have a mixture of types. Left: Flat roots.   Centre: Heart-shape.   Right: Tap-root.

and amino acids. In return, the fungi aid the tree's absorption of water and nutrients, and protect the roots from a number of diseases. The symbiosis of higher plants and fungi is called *mycorrhiza*.

The Trunk

The second movement of a germinating seed is directed towards the Sun (heliotropism). Tree trunks can grow to the top of the tree, for example, most needle-covered trees (conifers), or can spread into branches, such as most broadleaf (deciduous) trees. However, cross-sections of the trunks of both coniferous and deciduous trees reveal similar tissues.

— The cork or outer bark is the outermost shell of mature trees and consists of hard, dead tissue. It protects living, inner parts from weather, parasites and injury. With an increase in diameter the outer bark cracks and becomes grooved and rough. Eventually it comes off, either in scales (Norway Spruce, Apple tree), sheets (Yew, Pine), or papery strips (Birch, Cherry).

— The cork cambium is a thin layer of living cells that produces new cork to counteract external shedding and is vital for the tree's increase in diameter, since it protects the vulnerable inner layers.

— The bark is the outermost layer of young trees which have not yet produced cork. Beech and some birch trees are notable exceptions, retaining their bark for most of their lives, as it stretches smoothly with their increasing diameter.

— The inner bark (also bast or phloem) consists of living cells which form a system of pipelines. Food produced by the leaves generally moves downwards through the phloem to other parts of the tree (particularly the root system), but in early spring it moves upwards to the buds.

— The cambium is a layer of cells which is able to divide and rapidly produce two kinds of new cells: phloem cells on the outer side of the cambium, and new wood (xylem) on its inner side.

— In the xylem (sapwood) water and nutrients are transported upwards from the roots to the crown. The cells grow to a great length and then die. The xylem cells have a much bigger diameter than those of the phloem.

— The heartwood (or core) is the innermost part and consists of the parts of the xylem that have died off over many years. Water transport has stopped here. Heartwood often takes on a different colour from sapwood and helps the stability of the tree.

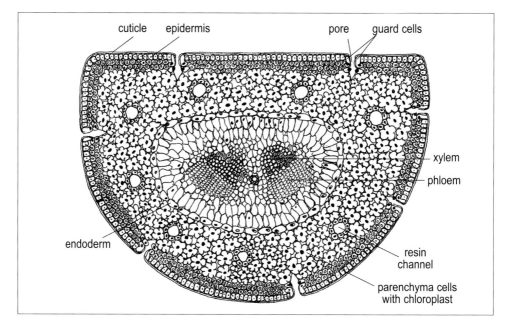

Figure 31. Section through a pine needle (magnified 80 times).

Annual rhythms — such as seasonal changes of light and temperature in the temperate zone, or rainy and dry seasons in the subtropics — are marked by rings which appear in the tree trunk. The tree's age can then be calculated by counting these annual rings — even the age of a particular branch can be determined. Favourable conditions for growth result in broader rings, and slight changes in the composition of the wood reveal a lot about weather and climatic conditions.

The crown

The crown is the most typical part of the tree, encompassing the branches, twigs, leaves, flowers and fruits.

The leaves manufacture food for the growth and development of the whole tree. From below they receive water and minerals; from above they receive sunlight and carbon dioxide from the air. Through the process of photosynthesis they produce carbohydrates (mainly sugars), which nourish the entire tree. Oxygen is actually a waste product of photosynthesis and is released into the air.

The veins in every leaf consist of two kinds of tube: the xylem (which transports water) and the phloem (which carries away the sap). Most of the

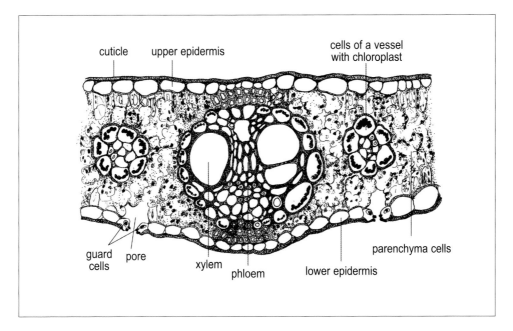

Figure 32. Section through a deciduous leaf.

cells inside the leaf have green bodies — *chloroplasts* — that contain chlorophyll, the central element of photosynthesis. Only a small part of the water
brought to the crown is used for the tree's metabolism. Most of it evaporates
through microscopic openings (the *stomata*) on the lower side of the leaves.
The transpiration of water and dissolved gases (oxygen and carbon dioxide)
occurs through these tiny pores.

A medium-sized deciduous tree has about two hundred thousand leaves.
This creates an enormous surface area for evaporation, similar to the alveoli
in our lungs. Thus a Beech with an average leaf surface of 20 cm² (3 sq.
inches) creates a transpiration and assimilation area of approximately
400 m² (480 sq. yards). A Beech tree can, therefore, transpire more than a
thousand litres of water on a summer's day.

The various hues of green in most leaves during spring and summer are
the result of chlorophyll. However, plant leaves also contain other pigments, such as *carotinoids*. With the onset of autumn, the tiny sap tubes in
the leaf stems begin to close, preventing further nutrition. The leaf begins to
die, the chlorophyll breaks down and these other pigments are revealed in
autumn reds and yellows which now appear.

Freestanding trees possess individual shapes which denote the typical
features of a species. In dense woodland, however, trees grow tall to absorb
sufficient amounts of light, thus they are less individual but still very

distinct (an oak wood, for example, has obvious differences from a maple or birch wood). When the shape of an individual tree mirrors the archetypal form of the species, it is sometimes referred to as the *alpha shape*.

Although the naturally diverse multitude of shapes is taken for granted, the reasons for the forms themselves remain a mystery to orthodox science, which is, however, able to explain the physical laws and metabolism of a form. Why are trees, leaves, buds, flowers and fruits so varied among different species? Botany is still looking for answers (see Chapter 5).

Growth

Apart from the diameter increase of the tree's limbs caused by the activity of the cambium, the tree also grows at the tips of its branches. Trees in the temperate zone develop buds during the summer. These can be wrapped in

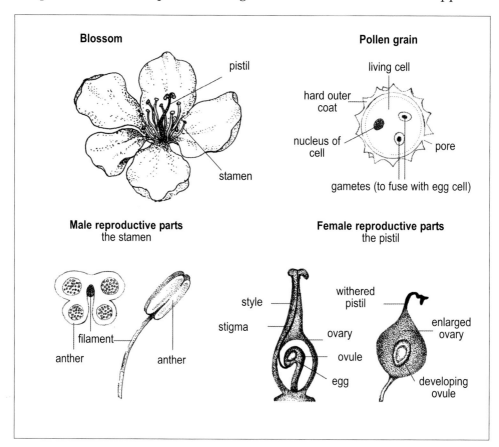

Figure 33. The reproductive organs.

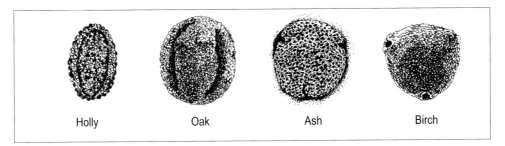

| Holly | Oak | Ash | Birch |

Figure 34. Pollen of different broadleaf trees.

bud scales to protect them from cold and dehydration during the winter. When warm weather arrives in the spring, the buds swell and burst open. The shoots begin to grow and thereby extend the volume of the crown. The rate of growth varies between species; a Horse Chestnut shoot can grow a foot or more, while a Yew twig only grows an inch or less.

In a mature tree the buds generally contain both flowers and leaves. In a few cases, for example, Elms, leaves and flowers develop from different kinds of buds.

Reproduction

Trees ensure the continuity of the species by means of sexual reproduction. Pollen from the male flower parts fertilizes the eggs in the female parts. This union produces fruits (seeds). Many broadleaf trees have flowers that contain both male and female organs. However, since nature prefers cross-fertilization to occur, all sorts of barriers are present to prevent a flower from self-fertilizing (Johnson 1973, 15). Thus, flowers need the co-operation of wind or insects to spread pollen.

Other trees, broadleaf as well as trees with needles, have separate male and female flowers (or cones in the case of conifers). These reproductive flowers either both grow on the same tree *(monoecious)* or on separate male and female trees *(dioecious)*. The latter kind particularly require the help of wind or insects for fertilization to take place.

In fruit-bearing trees *(angiosperms)* the ovule (later the seed) is enclosed by an ovary, which ripens into a fruit of various appearances: it can be soft and juicy (Cherry), hard (Oak, Hazel), or thin and winged (Birch, Elm, Ash).

Cone-bearing trees *(gymnosperms)* have unprotected ovules without an ovary. The biggest group among gymnosperms are conifers (pines, spruces, firs, cypresses, araucarias and a few others). In most of these species, each scale of a female cone contains two ovules. After pollination, the scales harden and the male gametes in each ovule unite with the female gametes. In most species, small seeds develop long wings, and these are scattered by the wind once the mature cone opens up.

The seed itself consists of a hard, protective shell, a sprout (embryo) and surrounding nutritious tissue (seed protein). Under the right conditions (soil, warmth, water and air) the seed grows into a new individual which resembles the parent plant.

Apart from these methods of reproduction some trees also have vegetative, non-sexual possibilities:

— SUCKERS. The roots of some trees can send up shoots that may grow into new trees, for example, Apple and Aspen.
— CUTTINGS. Twigs cut from some trees can be planted and will develop roots. This is usually done by people; however, a storm-damaged Willow tree might re-establish itself in this way.
— LAYERING. A very rare process by which branches reach down to the ground and take root. Eventually these roots may sprout and grow into an independent tree, as for example, with the Yew.

Adaptability

Climate

Conifers are generally well adapted to colder climates. Their needles have a thick outer layer that is coated with wax to reduce water loss. The sloping branches of the Norway Spruce easily shed snow, and its needles contain a type of anti-freeze to help them survive in areas of severe cold.

Deciduous trees employ a different strategy altogether to survive temperate winters. They shed their leaves in the autumn and hibernate during the cold season. As long as temperatures do not fall too low the tree is protected from frost by high quantities of stored sugars and starch; these also serve as initial food for the re-awakening tree in the spring. Imported tropical trees often die in the winter because they are unable to modify their stored reserve substances into a state with which they can counteract frost damage.

Weather

The tree shape is an ideal structure. Its life cycle shows astonishing signs of self-optimization:

— The leaves of all tree species (as of all tall plants) are coated with a thin layer of wax to prevent uncontrolled transpiration (water loss).

— Some trees, such as Oak, grow tiny hairs on the lower side of their leaves. This prevents too much air ventilation at the stomata and thus lowers the rate of transpiration.

— Stems keep leaves flexible; without them no tree could resist gale force winds.

— In response to wind pressure the trunk tapers upwards, having its greatest girth at the base where the greatest bending force occurs. Thus, the stress load is evenly distributed.

— When the wind forces the two parts of a forked tree apart, the fork itself suffers great tension stress. However, during its growth, the tree protects points of potential damage by laying down more wood at the higher stress points until the stress is as uniform as possible on the inside of the fork.

— The forks between trunk and branches, as well as between trunk and root, are of a similar design, and free from notch stress.

These defence mechanisms are supported by the choice of material itself. Wood consists of *cellulose,* which can resist traction forces to a high degree, and *lignin* which makes the wood pressure resistant. Scientists have discovered that the windward and leeward sides of trees contain different amounts of lignin. Thus the trunk reacts appropriately to pressure on one side, and traction on the other.

Injuries

A bark wound caused, for instance, by a carving or the feeding of a stag, disturbs the balance of the tree. This little notch can become a mechanical failure point in a storm as it destroys the carefully balanced distribution of lever arm forces that work on the tree. Although small, this notch can be the catalyst for serious mechanical damage or infection resulting from decay-causing organisms. The tree starts self-healing immediately; the cambium responds to new and excessively increased stresses and creates *callus* tissue (wound wood). The tree immediately begins to lay down a large amount of tissue to close the wound and relieve notch stress.

A special problem occurs when a whole branch dies, which can happen if it is too overshadowed by other branches. It would take years for bacteria and fungi to decompose this limb enough for it to break off. Only then can the cambium growth cover the wound. In the meantime the branch becomes a dangerous foreign body, as wood-decaying organisms it contains might spread and attack the whole tree. This is prevented by an accumulation of specialized substances at the base of that branch while it is dying, for example, resin in conifers and wound gum in deciduous trees. The slow decay of the dead limb also gives the tree enough time to adjust its gravitational arrangement in preparation for the falling branch altering the weight and balance of the whole tree.

Contact stress

If a stone, branch, fallen tree or barbed wire fence presses against the trunk this can also disturb the uniform load distribution. It can also lead to an injury by rubbing through the bark. New tissue soon wraps itself around the alien object, thus increasing the contact area and thereby reducing the contact stress by levelling it out. The fixation of the object furthermore prevents an open wound.

Age

The age of a tree is determined more by its size than by time. In the temperate zone trees usually form annual rings. On the inside the cambium creates wood cells which border those from the previous year. The material for this new wood is made by the leaves, and therefore the rate of a tree's growth depends largely on the ratio between the crown size and the surface area of trunk, branches and roots. When young, the height and crown of the tree increase vigorously each year. On reaching its maximum dimensions the tree enters middle age. After that, the crown no longer expands so much but the supporting structures (trunk, branches) still display a new annual ring. Eventually, the tree can no longer meet its commitments and branches start to die. The tree has now reached old age, but this is not necessarily a fatal condition.

The ability of a tree to prolong its life is determined by its capacity for *retrenchment* (see below) and recovering from damage, as well as the resistance of its heartwood against decay.

The best example of retrenchment is the *stag-headed* Oak, where old, upper branches have died and stick out from a new, smaller, active crown, that is in good health. In this way, older Oaks can live for many more decades. Elm trees too, can become very old, owing to their ability to recover from severe damage. Beech and Ash lack these qualities. The Beech tree is an icon of strength and firmness, but its wood is not durable; the absence of tannic acid (present in Oak) or resin (in conifers) makes it prone to early decay.

Even fast decaying wood can be counterbalanced by the capacity to regenerate itself after damage. Willow *pollards* are a characteristic example of this, as are the *coppice stools* of many trees, for example Ash and Hazel, where the ageing process begins again from the most recent cutting. Since coppice stools are completely self-renewing they can live almost indefinitely. Old stools spread into an external ring of living tissue with a decayed centre. Oliver Rackham found three-hundred-year-old Ash stools, two to five feet across, and one of nearly nineteen feet in width, which:

> may be one of the oldest living things in Britain (at least a thousand years) but still yields a good crop of poles. (Rackham 1976, 29)

Coppicing and pollarding have existed since the Bronze Age, but were of particular importance during the Middle Ages, when small pieces of woodland were used as sustainable resources. In coppicing, young trees are cut close to the ground every four to ten years. For most species this stimulates new growth and vital new shoots. Hazel responds particularly well to coppicing and its individual lifespan is even prolonged by this treatment. Oak, Willow and Elm in pastureland were *pollarded* rather than *coppiced;* their branches being cut about six or seven feet above the ground, thus preventing new shoots from being eaten by cattle.

The supreme example of slow growth and longevity is the Yew tree (see pages 224f).

A general rule for estimating the age of a free standing tree is to allow one inch of girth — measured at about 1.5 m (five feet) above the ground — for every year of its age; allow half an inch for a tree in a wood. This gives average annual ring widths of four and two millimetres respectively, and works well with naturally grown (not pollarded or coppiced) trees in youth and middle age (with the exception of Yew). However, it should be remembered, that most trees grow faster when young, and more slowly when old.

Unfortunate environmental conditions can also considerably slow down a tree's growth. A small tree on a stand that is poor in light, water and nutrients can be older than a giant in an excellent position. Pollarding makes it nearly impossible to tell how old a tree is. Oliver Rackham found Oak pollards in Epping Forest, Essex, with a girth of fifty inches that were at least 350 years old:

> having maintained an average ring width of 0.4 mm since 1720; this must be close to the slowest rate at which an oak can grow and yet remain alive. Oaks which are much retrenched in old age probably grow at about this rate. (Rackham 1976, 27)

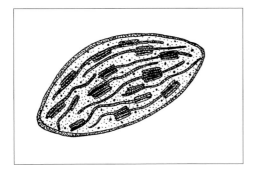

Figure 35. Chloroplast.
(After Devlin & Witham).

Photosynthesis

Chloroplasts have been called the most important organelles for sustaining all life, because of their ability to collect light energy and convert it to chemical energy, through the process of photosynthesis.

The inside of the chloroplast is called the *stroma*. The inner membrane forms long folds within the stroma, which are called *lamellae*. Other membranes, resembling miniature pancakes, are called *grana*, and are usually gathered in stacks, attached to the lamellae. It is here that the photochemical reactions of photosynthesis take place. The various molecules and substances, which are vital for photosynthesis, are located inside these membranes, including chlorophyll, the pigment that gives all higher plants their green colour.

In photosynthesis the membranes of the chloroplasts catch light and after a series of complicated chemical processes finally create carbohydrates. Experiments have shown that photosynthesis causes a considerable energy rise of 1,200 mV within the leaf cells (Mengel 1991).

Figure 36.
The centre of
chloroplast. (After
Devlin & Witham).

The xylem

The xylem is the tube system which transports the water containing inorganic, soluble ions (nutrients) into the crown. The evaporation of water molecules through the pores in the leaves creates suction, thus forcing the molecules next to them to move up and fill the abandoned spaces. This continues throughout the water stream, connecting evaporation areas above ground with subterranean ground water. In this way intense transpiration causes intense water absorption activity by the roots.

Air humidity and temperature affect transpiration. Wind enhances it by carrying away moist air, thus the characteristics of the air influence the tree's metabolism.

Of course, not all water evaporates. Young cells need water for growth. The xylem branches out and spreads into each leaf, creating contact points with other living tissues, which take water from it by means of osmosis. This happens mainly at night, when suction forces from the stomata are not as strong as during the day.

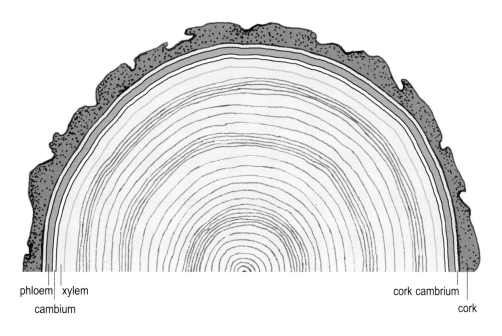

phloem xylem   cork cambrium
     cambium   cork

Figure 37. Cross section of a tree trunk.

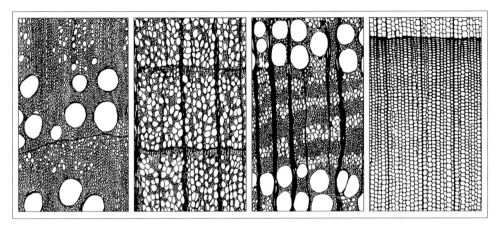

Figure 38. Cross-sections of (left to right): Oak, Beech, Elm, Spruce. (After Stern).

When they have reached their destined shape and size the xylem cells die. The inner core (or protoplast) which contains everything within the cell wall, including the cell membrane, vanishes, and only the thick, strong walls of cellulose remain. In fact, single tubes occasionally implode in extremely hot and dry weather, which can be recognised by an audible cracking noise from inside the trunk. However, trees produce new xylem annually, through the work of the cambium, and thereby augment their capacity for water transport. At the same time, older xylem tubes gradually become blocked and, after undergoing some chemical changes, only function as supporting tissue. As every tree species has its own rhythms, proportions and characteristics these structures look very different from each other.

The phloem

The phloem is the other long-distance transport system of trees and other complex plants. Its extension and branching equals that of the xylem, but it does not work as the result of a vacuum, but through pressure which pushes sap through the tubes.

Phloem sap is more concentrated than the solution in the xylem, and its most common component is sucrose. Sucrose and other sugars are of vital significance because they are the most effective means of transporting organic carbohydrates, which are important carriers and suppliers of energy. Carbon is the dominant building material in plant organisms.

There is another difference from the xylem: phloem cells are living cells, and have very thin cell walls. There are actually two main types of phloem cells; *sieve* cells and *companion* cells. The long sieve cells are the actual transport cells, and are connected, forming continuous channels (sieve tubes). At the contact area of two sieve cells they develop a corresponding pattern of pores, which are reinforced by a special substance called sieve plates. The *cytoplasm*, which contains everything within the cell membrane except the cell nucleus, is confined to a thin layer along the sieve tube membrane to give space to the passing sap. Even the nucleus retreats and disappears completely (see Figure 39). This is remarkable because normally no cell can survive without its nucleus, which contains all necessary information. It is made possible by the companion cells, whose nuclei supply the sieve cells with the control functions they need for their metabolism. Each sieve cell is coupled with at least one companion cell.

It is not known for certain how the phloem creates its pressure. The *mass flow hypothesis* gives the most likely explanation and has been proved by experiments. It states that osmosis creates excessive pressure at the upper end of the system. Initially, sugars produced by photosynthesis are pumped into the phloem against the concentration gradient. Once they are inside the phloem, water from intercellular spaces follows easily, simply because of the laws of osmosis. This pressure is then exerted downwards, allowing the root to take sugar and water from the phloem, and keeping the pressure low at the bottom end of the system. Sugar and other nutrients in the sap serve as food for the root, and also create energy stores for the winter and especially the spring. Interestingly, at least part of the water is reabsorbed by the xylem through which it rises again.

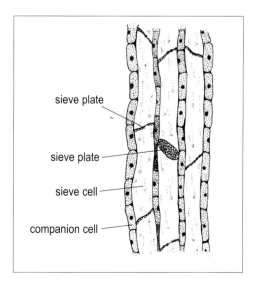

Figure 39. The phloem structure.

Unlike the xylem the direction of flow in the phloem is reversible. This is important in the spring when the reawakening tree mobilizes the energy stored in the roots and trunk before its metabolism is fully producing food again.

When a phloem tube is injured the sieve plates react immediately by shutting it down, because sap generally has the highest concentrations of nutrients within the plant, and its loss has to be kept to the absolute minimum.

Birch

Birch family: *Betulaceae*
Silver Birch *(Betula pendula)*
Downy Birch *(Betula pubescens)*

Physical appearance

The Birch is named after the unique whiteness of its bark, from the Old High German word *bircha* (shining white). This is caused by tiny grains of betulin, a crystalline pigment found in the *vacuole* (storage space for sugars, starch and other chemicals) of bark cells. This white, horizontally striped, papery, peeling bark with its black diamond-shaped markings is the best means of identifying of the Silver Birch and the similar Hairy Birch. Birch needs a lot of light and the tree itself appears airy and full of light. The friendly Birch brightens up the dark solitude and heaviness of the north.

Its delicate twigs always respond readily to the wind. The light foliage consists of small oval or triangular, sharply pointed leaves with a doubly toothed edge, which are bright green in the spring, and turn yellow in the autumn. In the winter, the twigs are purple. Birch wood is tough and flexible, but rots quickly. The bark, however, is much more durable.

Birch is one of the first trees to colonize wastelands. It can grow on hard rock, poor sand and acid moorland; its shallow root system indicates that not much is expected of the soil. The few minerals it needs are broken down and made accessible to the tree by fungi.

The female catkins mature in the summer and eventually release myriads of small, broadly winged nutlets, which are carried away by the wind and can swiftly colonize wide areas. Only in the early stages of succession can birches create dense woodlands. Their favourite companions are grasses, and later, when the soil allows it, other trees, such as Oak. Since Birch trees do not get very old (eighty to one hundred years, rarely reaching one hundred and twenty), and because many seedlings whither under the mother trees, time and time again Birch gives way to other tree species, after having enhanced the soil for their benefit. All of this shows the character of birch: coming and going like the wind, creating space for other trees.

Healing

Birch has always been a very important tree in temperate and arctic zones. In Asia, Europe and America its durable bark was used for boats, canoes and containers. It was even tanned to make buckets and shoes. The bark contains birch tar, which makes birch wood combustible even when freshly cut. A Russian proverb says the Birch gives light (bark rolled for torches), calms screams (tar for smearing on cart wheels), heals (see below) and cleanses (branches used for beating the body in saunas). The Ojibwa Native Americans also used Birch in sweat lodge *cleansing* ceremonies, and covered their tepees with it; while in Europe, it was sometimes used for roof tiles.

As Birch works with the water system in nature, it also works with the water system in the human body. Tea made from the young leaves and birch sap stimulates the gallbladder, kidneys and bladder. They are generally diuretic, antiseptic and slightly sudorific (creates fever). The blood-cleansing sap is a time-honoured tonic for the whole metabolism. When taken internally Birch has a mild anti-depressant effect as well. It also brings spiritual flexibility and softness to those tending to stiffness and rigidity, and is beneficial for diseases such as arthritis and rheumatism. Birch water is a well-known external tonic for the scalp.

The homeopathic essence, *Betula alba,* is described as having rejuvenating, cleansing and comforting properties, and brings life and light into dark, old or sick environments.

For a general body 'spring clean,' gather the young leaves in April and May. Two, three or four cups of the tea should be drunk daily for about three weeks. It is up to personal taste how many leaves you use per cup.

The young leaves are also a healthy addition to fresh salads.

Tradition

Birch has always been considered as *the tree of the beginning.* It prepares the Earth as well as the soul. The first versions of the ancient Indian *Vedas* were written on birch bark, and in ancient Ireland, the 'mother of learning' (as Birch was sometimes called) presides over the alphabet: the first letter b (beth) represents the Birch. Curiously, in the Jewish Kabbalah, the term *beth* is also associated with the beginning. In Hebrew, *beth* denotes the 'two' of

Birch.

Birch wood.

Kabbalistic numerology, which stands for the power that 'opens creation's process of taking form' (Weinreb 1980, 222).

In Irish mythology, the first ogham signs were carved into Birch, to warn the light god, Lugh, that his wife was about to be kidnapped by the underworld:

> ... on the birch was written the first ogham inscription that was brought into Ireland, to wit, thy wife will be taken from thee ... unless thou watch her. It is on that account b is still written at the beginning of the ogham alphabet (Calder 1917, 91).

The protection of Birch is a strong characteristic of many customs all over Europe. Cradles of birch wood were meant to protect babies from bad influences, for example, in fairy tales the threat of fairies swapping a baby for a changeling. The birch broom was more than a practical domestic tool. It was ritually used to brush out the *spirit* of the old year to make space for the new. Then it was hung from the apex of the roof or above the door as a protection charm.

The tender, graceful Birch was sacred to Frigga, wife of Odin (originally a wind god), and later, herbalists and alchemists associated Birch with Frigga's Roman equivalent, Venus. Spring and fertility rites and festivities took place in Birch groves, which were regarded as earthly manifestations of the goddess of love. Not so long ago, Scottish lads and maidens still paired off to the Birch groves at Beltane, while adults were free of marriage vows for that one day. An old Welsh poem goes:

> Is it true, the girl that I love,
> That you do not desire the birch,
> The strong growth of summer?
> Be not a nun in spring,
> Ascetism is not as good as a bush ...
> Come to the spreading birch
> To the religion of the trees and the cuckoo. (Fife 1994)

The Church did not approve of this. Not long after they had stopped the population of most European countries from engaging in these sinful deeds, the people simply turned it around. Instead of going out to the grove, they brought a Birch tree into the village, decorated it colourfully and held a spring festival around it — the maypole appeared in the thirteenth century. The Church did not give up. Birch sprays were brought into churches for Whitsun decorations, and gradually Birch customs took on a Christian aspect. A Russian Whitsun custom clearly reveals its pre-Christian origins: a small Birch tree is ceremonially brought to the house, festively decorated and honoured for three days as the spirit of life and returning vegetation.

In Siberian shamanism, Birch is the World Tree itself, and is honoured as the 'deity of the door,' who helps the shaman to cross into the spirit world and also guides his passage back to this world (Wirth 1979).

Celtic chieftains of the German Halstatt period were buried with a small conical birch bark hat, which is believed to represent the guardian of passage and a proud warrior's submission to the cosmic mother, entrusting himself to her in death and rebirth.

Inspiration

Birch represents the part of the universal soul described in myth by many names — Frigga, Demeter, Aphrodite, Venus — the divine mother and goddess of love. Birch also gave its name to the Germanic rune *berkana* meaning motherhood, bosom, and protection. The shape of the rune is derived from

The Germanic rune Berkana.

the Neolithic breasts of Mother Earth (Wirth 1979). The Irish goddess of re-turning light, Brigid, bears in her name a clear link to *bhereg*, the etymolog-ical Indo-European root of Birch.

It is not surprising that the ogham symbol that warned Lugh was carved on birch: Birch itself *is* his wife, the partner of the light god, and by bring-ing the warning on birch she is already safely united with him.

Birch is the incarnation of the White Goddess (see also Hawthorn). When climate changes Birch scatters her seeds over the vast tundra, moors and wastelands, to bring life back. Her physical body might appear soft and humble, but Birch is at one with the most powerful force of the universe, that of unconditional love.

Rowan

Rose family: *Rosaceae*
Rowan, Mountain Ash, Quicken-tree (*Sorbus aucuparia*)

Physical appearance

The Rowan belongs to the Rose family, like Wild Rose and Hawthorn, rarely growing higher than 13.5 m (45 feet). It does not dominate its space, letting light through its crown, and does not require much of the soil. It, therefore, allows other plants to grow around and beneath it.

The creamy white compound inflorescence (shoots bearing clusters of flowers), consist of bisexual flowers with five petals, which open in late May. These develop into berries, which change from green to orange, and in the autumn become bright scarlet. The Rowan is a wild fruit tree found in the colder parts of the temperate zone and provides food for birds, particularly the thrush. The abundance of its fruits, however, depends on the amount of accessible light. The Rowan sacrifices size for the production of food.

There are two main habitats for this hardy, frost-resistant tree: on hillsides and lower mountain slopes up to 1,800 m (5,900 feet), where, in the Alps, for example, the dark mass of Spruce needs to be broken up. Here, Rowan balances the soil by aiding the transformation of slowly decomposing needles into fertile humus.

Its German name, *Eberesche*, is widely believed to mean 'false Ash,' but it is more likely that the word derives from the Gaulish *eburos* (Yew), Middle High German *esche* and the Old High German *ask* (Ash), because it has feathered leaves similar to the Ash and berries as red as the fruits of the Yew.

Leaves and berries of the Rowan.

Healing

The bitter berries are — contrary to common belief — not poisonous, although the seeds inside the berries contain parasorbic acid, which upsets
the stomach and metabolism. No more than eight or ten berries should be
eaten raw.

Apart from sorbitannic acid and other organic acids rowan berries contain sugar, carotin, pectin, essential oil, vitamin A and more vitamin C than
oranges and lemons. Thus, they generally strengthen the immune system,
cleanse the blood and are anti-rheumatic.

Rowan also has a balancing effect on the digestive system. The dried
berries and leaves are known to help in case of gastritis and diarrhoea (Leaf
tea: two teaspoons of dried leaves per cup; two cups daily). The raw or
cooked berries have a slightly laxative and diuretic effect, and are also an old
remedy for stimulating and cleansing the kidneys, as well as helping with
coughs and throat inflammations (5–8 dried berries eaten during the day, or
a gargle can be made from the tea of the berries). Singers and speakers value

them for keeping the vocal cords smooth. A tea made from the flowers is also an old remedy against coughs and bronchitis. Walkers pick single berries because they quench the thirst and refresh.

Since boiling destroys parasorbic acid, the most delicious way to enjoy Rowan is as rowan jelly. The gathered berries are washed, weighed and brought to the boil. To make it go further, elderberries or small pieces of apple or pear can be added (one third or even half of the rowan berries weight). This dilutes the rowanberries' bitterness, which especially newcomers to this taste particularly welcome. Once boiling it is possible to shorten the boiling time by crushing the hard, waxed shells with a potato masher. After a good five minutes of gentle boiling brown sugar can be added, the same weight as the fruit. Beginners might want it sweeter and should use one and a third times the amount of sugar than fruit. After stirring it well the pectin can be added. Put the jelly into sterile jars, seal and allow to cool.

Juice and wine made from rowanberries are also delicious. For both, pour boiling water over 2 kg (4.5 lb) of clean, stalk-less berries. Cover the bowl and leave to stand for four days. For juice, the berries are then crushed, and the liquid is strained. Sugar (twice the weight of the berries) is cooked to syrup together with the strained liquid, and poured into bottles. For wine, the berries are not crushed, only the extracted juice is strained. Add sugar in the same proportion as for the jelly, plus 250 g (8 oz) of raisins and the juice of three lemons. Stir it all together, and add the mixture to already activated wine yeast. Cover the open (this is important!) vessel with a clean cloth and let it stand for another two weeks. Then strain into a fermentation jar to develop as with any other wine.

The most important factor is to choose a tree to pick fruit from that is far enough away from all sources of air pollution.

Tradition

Rowan has been one of the most venerated trees in northwest Europe, surpassing even Beech and Oak. This was most apparent in Scotland, where:

> ... tradition does not allow the use of the tree's timber, bark, leaves or flowers, nor the cutting of these, except for sacred purposes under special conditions (Fife 1994).

The cutting, carrying, and placing of rowan twigs above doorways, for protection against misfortune, was formerly part of special rituals. In

Rowan and its connections with divination, music and bards.

Scotland, the Rowan symbolized death and the after-life, being a medium between this world and the next, and its wood was burnt only for funeral pyres or divination. It did, however, play a part in the ceremonial baking of sacred cakes, for which the grain was prepared using a threshing tool made of rowan wood.

Rowan was considered as a protection against spells or anything evil. The Rowan's ability to grow where soil seems non-existent, such as in the forks of other trees or on bare rock, only added to its supernatural image. Growing on another tree further reinforced its qualities as a being not belonging to Earth or Heaven, like Mistletoe.

In Ireland, Rowan is associated with Brigid, the muse of the arts, spinning and weaving. The traditional material for spindles and spinning wheels is rowan wood. An ancient tale mentions Druids burning rowan wood for divination and to invoke spirit beings, while other Celtic sources indicate Rowan's important role in the cleansing ceremonies of the spring festival, Beltane. It furthermore seems that Druids planted rowan trees at sacred sites such as stone circles.

The muse sent her rowan arrows of inspiration not only to the Irish bards, but also to the early medieval bards of Wales who carved their runes in rowan trees. This can also be assumed of Norse peoples, particularly those who lived in parts of Iceland where Rowan was the only tree. The Rowan shares its Old Icelandic name *runa* (secret; to whisper) with the runes.

An old pagan custom that lived on until modern times in various parts of Europe, was the annual use of the *Life Rod* in the spring, which was believed to carry the spirit of the returning vegetation. Every human, animal, and even orchard trees were *beaten* with it, and thus blessed with the gifts of life, health, fertility and good luck. In some areas the rod was taken from Willow or Hazel, but the dominant life tree was the Rowan, as indicated by its oldest names: Anglo-Saxon *cvicbeam*, from *cvic* (life). This root is reflected in Rowan's other name, *Quicken-tree*, indicating sharing out the blessings of life.

This tree was so associated with the source of life that the only Irish mythical image, that clearly denotes the Tree of Life, is based on Rowan. In the story of Diarmuid and Grania the lovers flee from the revenge of Fionn, leader of the Fianna, and come to the wood of Dubhros. In its depth grows a wonderful Quicken-tree. When the elves were once passing that wood one of their musicians dropped a 'berry of the Land of the Ever-Living Ones.' Seeing the rare 'beautiful Druid tree' that had grown from it, the elves decided that the tree should be guarded, and had found Searbhan Lochlannach, the Surly One of Lochlann, for this task. This peculiar gigantic, black and ugly man, with crooked teeth, one eye, and a mighty iron club guarded the tree day and night. No mortal was allowed to steal one of its berries. The berries were intoxicating and rejuvenating, 'any old person of a hundred years that would eat them would go back to be young again.' (see Lady Gregory 1970, 286). Diarmuid and Grania hide in the quicken-tree and eat its berries, while Fionn and four hundred warriors of the Fianna, who want to kill the lovers, surround the foot of the tree. Their escape is finally made possible by Angus Og, a powerful spirit being and Diarmuid's mentor, who makes Grania vanish and takes her with him to the Otherworld, from the tree top where she was hiding — a deed unmistakably denoting the tree as a gate between the worlds.

The Quicken-tree of Dubhros could be interpreted as a Yew rather than a Rowan because of its red berries, but the themes of health (vitamin C), young lovers (fertility), music and above all, protection, clearly point to the Rowan.

In Norse myth, this theme of protection even includes the god, Thor. In Icelandic legend he nearly drowns in a river but is able to grab the branch of a Rowan tree to pull himself out. Since Thor (called Donar by southern Germanic tribes) governs thunder and lightning, associations of Rowan and lightning can be found in many places where these tribes once settled, for example, Bohemia, Saxony and northern England. Rowan twigs were generally believed to provide protection from lightning, and in terms of natural science, the Rowan is one of the species most rarely struck by lightning. (Stäubli 1927).

Even the Christian era could not diminish the fame of Rowan. In Wales, for example, a piece of rowan bark was a talisman against witches, conjurers, sorcerers and the devil, and against any spell or evil. It was considered lucky to have a Rowan growing near the home. '... the berries brought into the house were followed by prosperity and success. A bunch of the berries worn in girdle or bodice kept women from being bewitched' (Trevelyan 1909, 103). Similar reports have also appeared from Christian England, Ireland and Poland.

Inspiration

The recurrent theme in all these tales is obviously *protection*. By cleansing our blood Rowan also cleanses our soul and attitudes; energies that in tribal times were called bad luck or spells, while in the Christian era they were termed *witches* and *demons*.

Rowan's connection with divination, music and bards points to its ability to channel higher inspiration to humankind. Thus Rowan, known among

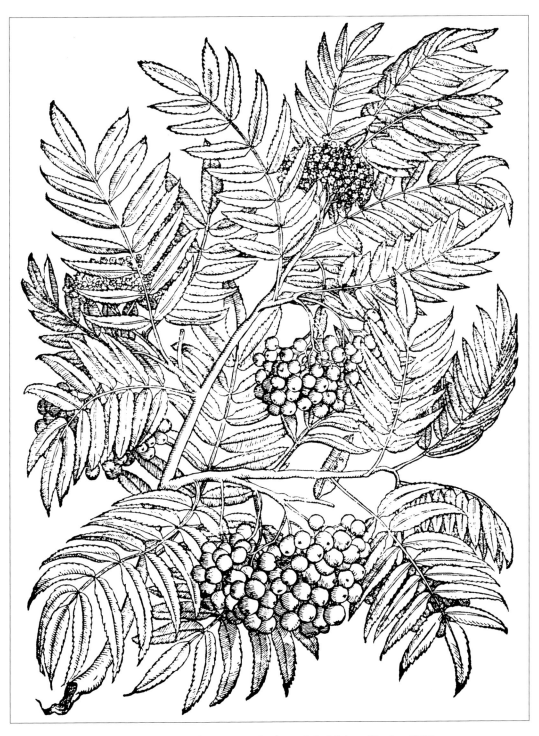

Rowan twig and berries. Etching by Petrus Andreas Mathiolus, Venice 1565.

modern Druids as the Tree of the Bards opens our higher senses to subtle processes and connects us with the realms above. It makes us resistant to the spells of the world by connecting us more strongly with our Higher Self, the source of true, authentic inspiration; only by truly being ourselves are we protected from losing ourselves to seductions or enchantments.

This is also expressed in the Thor legend. Rudolf Steiner described Thor as the archangel who brought the powers of will power and self-awareness, to the people. So, by rescuing Thor, Rowan helps to maintain the independence and individuality of the conscious self.

Consequently, Rowan has always been considered as one of the most powerful talismans, mighty enough even to guard the soul through the passage of death. A rowan twig was found in a medicine pouch in a Bronze Age tomb in Sweden. Traditionally, the only tree that has shared the tasks of the Yew in Welsh graveyards is the Rowan.

Rowan, which follows Birch in the Irish tree alphabet, mediates the Inner Voice, which knows our own destiny and potential, allowing us to develop with a sense of our own individuality and faith in the higher purpose of life here on Earth. The gift of Rowan is the gift of inspiration, and not only for bards: all of us can bring creativity to ordinary parts of our lives.

Ash

Olive family: *Oleaceae*
Common Ash (*Fraxinus excelsior*)

Physical appearance

The Ash is recognized by its paired, feathered leaves, the leaflets of which are shallowly toothed. The tree prefers well-watered stands which it shares with Alder or, in upper parts of river valleys, with Lime and various species of Elm and Sycamore. The Ash can be found in wide parts of Europe and North America but prefers moist soil and air; a fact that, in Europe, makes it more common in the British Isles than in the drier continental climate. In Ireland, Ash and Hawthorn are the two most common trees found at sacred springs. Ash is fully-grown after about one hundred years and generally reaches about three times that age, although far older trees are also known.

The Ash loves light, and it lets light pass through its bright green foliage creating reflections and shadows like no other tree. As it reaches into the light so it reaches into the darkness below; long, far-reaching, flat roots send out a dense network of fine roots. As a result of this and the nutritious foliage it sheds annually, it is important in humus production, and it breaks down and ventilates the soil.

Ash trees are male, female or hermaphrodite. They flower in April to May, long before the leaves unfold. The flowers are a mixed form: they are like catkins (Willow, Poplar), but have bigger single blossoms, and ultimately turn into flat, winged nutlets similar to Maple and Elm. These nutlets usually hang in bunches on the tree all winter long, to be scattered by the March winds.

Thus the Ash contains the best qualities of the many different trees: soft and firm; fast and persistent; graceful and strong; linear and round. A German saying calls the Oak the king, and the Ash the high king among the trees.

Healing

In the fourth century BC the Greek physician Hippocrates used Ash preparations to cure gout and rheumatism. Nearly all the herbal books since the Middle Ages refer to the healing properties of the Ash. The bark, leaves and seeds are generally diuretic, laxative, blood-cleansing and help to loosen the salts of uric acid. The seeds also strengthen the liver and spleen. Until the nineteenth century, the inner side of the bark was known as a remedy for healing bleeding wounds. As a first-aid cure it is gently placed on to the wound; the fresh sap acts as a disinfectant. The leaves, for their part, refresh the tired feet of the rambler when put inside shoes.

For internal use, four teaspoons of dried leaves or seeds can be boiled with two cups of water, then strained and drunk during the day. The seeds can also be applied externally to soothe rheumatic pains or simple muscle ache. To make *Ash spirit* the seeds are mixed in equal parts with Juniper berries and leaves of Melissa and Peppermint. This is then covered with alcohol and left by a sunny window for three weeks (shake occasionally). Then the *spirit* is poured into a dark coloured bottle and can be rubbed into aching body parts. The ash wood also has blood-cleansing properties.

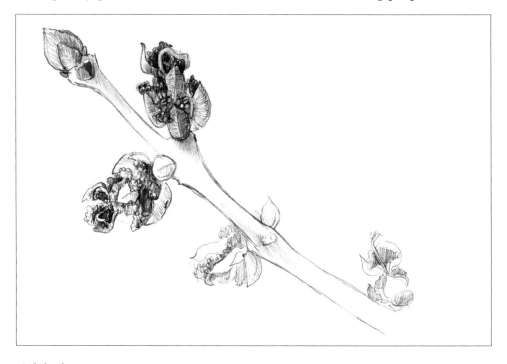

Ash buds.

The very young, sticky leaves can be used to enrich the taste of salads in May and June.

Those who wish to use the Ash for a ceremonial beverage can follow an old Germanic custom, and leave spring water overnight in an ash cup or chalice, and drink it the next day.

Like the herbal preparations from this tree, the homeopathic remedy, *Fraxinus excelsior*, also relieves the symptoms of gout and rheumatism.

Tradition

In Old Norse mythology — the *Eddas* — *ask* and *embla* appear as the trees from which mankind was created; woman from Elm and man from Ash. In Classical Greece, the present, 'third or brazen race of man' was considered to be 'the fruit of the Ash.' The Ash herself, *Melia*, was the daughter of Oceanus, and married the river-god, Inachos. Then Mother Ash gave birth to Phoroneus, the fire-bringer and first man (Folkard 1892).

For millennia the Ash was seen as benevolent to young life. In Scotland, the vigour with which Ash supports itself was widely recognized and Ash was considered to have a benign influence on the newborn. People used to give the sap of the tree to newly born babies, and to put green ash twigs on the birth chamber fire: 'in honour of the tree and as a prayer made for the newborn child' (Fife 1994).

In England, and on the continent, customs based on the tree's ability to heal were still alive in the nineteenth century. In Sweden, the Ash was one of the *Varträd*, the guardian trees of the farm or estate, and the Ash Woman (*Askafroa*) was honoured with regular offerings of milk or beer. Ash trees, however, were not planted close to the house or crops, because their vigorous root system can damage stonewalls or hinder the growth of crops.

Ash is generally considered to have power over water. Ancient Celtic customs incorporated ash wood in boats, to prevent them from sinking. In the great migration of the nineteenth century, most Irish people carried a piece of Ash over the Atlantic. From the other end of Europe Graves reports that Ash was used in rain-making ceremonies in prehistoric Greece, where for a long time the *meliae*, the Ash nymphs, were considered to have originally been cloud spirits and daughters of mighty sea gods, 'whose domain was originally the cloud sea' (Folkard 1892, 7). Later, the Greeks dedicated the Ash to the Sun and to Poseidon, the god of the sea.

The Ash has male and female aspects in its actual physical appearance. It exists as dioecious (separate male and female trees), as well as monoecious trees (with male, female or hermaphrodite flowers on the same tree), and this is reflected in the historical and mythological context. The female side of Ash is connected with life-giving waters, birth, healing and protection. The male side of the sacred tree is regarded as the *omphalos* (centre of the universe), the wand or the spear.

Although the five sacred trees of Ireland were originally derived from Yew, it is commonly believed that two or three of them were Ash. It is quite possible as the Ash is botanically a strong tree in Ireland. It seems that some of the ancient Yews were later replaced by Ash trees.

With the increasing alienation of the Europeans from the spiritual dimension of nature their awareness of trees changed, too. It was not only the Irish who changed their sacred trees in this way, but also the descendants of the Germanic tribes: Odin's ancient World (Yew) Tree, *Yggdrasil*, became the 'World Ash.'

One thing, however, was always made of Ash: Odin's spear, and indeed any spear made by Iron Age peoples, whether Germanic or not. The Greek centaur Chiron, for example, manufactured a spear from Ash which gave Achilles his legendary victory. Greeks and Romans, as well as Germanic and Celtic tribes, had spears and also arrows made from Ash.

However, ash sticks did not only bring death. Druids' wands were often made of Ash; a famous wand from Anglesey (first century BC) carrying a spiral ornamentation in a clockwise direction. The Ash's Old Irish name *nion* links it with Nuada of the Silver Hand, a king of the elfin race of the *Tuatha Dé Danann,* and also his ancient British counterpart, *Nodens*, to whom a large healing sanctuary on the River Severn was dedicated in the third to fifth centuries. Both their names are interpreted as 'cloud-maker' (Green 1992, 162).

Inspiration

It is no accident that Ash is the third tree in the original ogham (tree alphabet): after birth (Birch) and the awakening of individuality (Rowan) we start our relationship with the world around us. Ash is the tree that connects, bringing together the creative, male, solar ray and the receptive, fertile waters of life. It thus becomes a nurse of the newly born.

Spears and arrows are expressions of will power. When these hit the eternal ocean of possibilities creation takes place. Therefore Ash is also the tree of the magicians. Ash is the trident of the sea-gods Manawyddan/Mananaan (Welsh/Irish) and Poseidon. Ash gives power in this world, which is why Iron Age warriors preferred ash spears to the Neolithic yew spears.

Light filtering through Ash's foliage.

The presence of Ash stimulates the imagination, gives daring ideas, and invokes a thirst for action.

The Ash serves in the interplay of Sun and water, but the tree's secret is not the heart of the fire, or the depth of the water, but the connection between them. The Spirit of Ash connects, links and bridges — the inner and the outer world, above and below, far and near, male and female.

A crooked Ash.

Alder

Birch family: *Betulaceae*
Common Alder *(Alnus glutinosa)*

Physical appearance

Alder is found near lakes, rivers and in wetlands. Single trees can become quite gnarled, but in a group they shoot up high and can be moderately old. Its light foliage allows a rich accompanying growth of buck's beard, meadowsweet, ground-elder and touch-me-not. This in turn attracts a multitude of insects and thus the fertile, vibrant, lush green space beneath the Alder offers food and shelter to many animal species: finches, water-fowl, otter, badger and many kinds of frogs, as well as fish. Often this tree also blends into mixed woodlands, for example with Ash, Sycamore and Elm.

The roots take hold deep in wet ground. They can bind and enliven the wet soil in places that other trees avoid because of oxygen deficiency. Beside streams, alders sometimes reveal naked roots which protect the banks from erosion. Root symbioses allow Alder to bind nitrogen from the air. The high nitrogen content of this tree also reveals itself in the autumn through the grey-blackish colours which appear on the leaves. By shedding this nutritious foliage nitrogen and the other minerals are passed on to the undergrowth. As a result of this and the tree's ability to strengthen, ventilate and drain the soil, Alder prevents wetlands from turning into bog or marsh. In places that are too boggy or poor in nutrients the Downy Birch takes its place.

Alder bark is smooth and greenish-brown at first, but later becomes fissured and very dark brown or grey. The wood is reddish and when freshly cut turns orange-red. It is most durable when constantly wet, which is why it has been used for bridges, pumps, sluices and piles for medieval cathedrals. Venice is still said to rest partly on ancient alder piles.

Alder matures after about thirty years. Each spring it unfolds both sex of flower on one tree (monoecious). After flowering, leaves appear which are sticky when young, hence its Latin name *glutinosa* (sticky). The hanging male catkins reveal that is a plant of the birch family, although the female

Alder in winter.

catkins later turn into woody cones, which is a rather unusual design for the fruits of a temperate leaf tree. Many of these dark, oval cones persist on the tree through the winter while the winged nutlets fly off or float away on the water — they are equipped with tiny air bags for this purpose — to germinate on another bank downstream.

Healing

In the past, Alder was used in many ways: the bark for tanning leather; bark or leaves for dye; the wood for charcoal production; and fresh spring twigs were used to sweep the floor in the hope that fleas would stick to the leaves. The wood is rarely used for building, as woodworm loves its protein-rich substance.

The leaves and bark are astringent and antiseptic and can be used as a gargle in cases of inflammation of the mouth (two teaspoons should be boiled for five minutes in one cup of water). Bark preparations were used to heal rashes or festering wounds.

In homeopathy, the bark tincture of an American species, *Alnus rubra*, acts mainly on the mucous membranes, skin and glands. It is used for chronic skin infections, rheumatism, syphilis and urinary tract infections, as well as an aid to digestion.

Alder by Martin Klatt.

Tradition

Since the time of the ancient Greeks there is written evidence that humans believed that trees bled when cut. However, the Alder does indeed bleed! The sap turns red when it comes into contact with air. Thus this tree was always surrounded with a strong air of mystique, but also affection. It stands mostly in wet areas and is therefore often treated as a creature of the mist; a world in which people never feel comfortable, particularly because mist and twilight can inspire extraordinary imaginations in people's minds.

Unfortunately, there is little evidence of the spiritual role of Alder in pre-Christian times. The medieval *Wulfdietrich Saga* gives a strong idea of Alder Woman. In various local German legends she appears to wanderers as a seductive woman teaching wanton males a lesson by turning into a hairy or bark-like creature once in their embrace. Her different German names — *Else, Elsa, Elise* — are derived from the Anglo-Saxon *alor*, or the Gothic (of the Goths) *alisa* (alder), and do not stem, as commonly believed, from the Hebrew *Elizabeth*.

In the second song of the *Wulfdietrich Saga* the Rough Else, a wild-looking woman of the woods who is covered in hair, puts a spell on the hero eventually making him mad. He runs wildly through the woods, living on herbs for six months. Then she takes him on a ship over the sea to another land where she is queen. She bathes in a magical well that washes away her rough skin, and is transformed into the most beautiful of women and has a new name — *Sigeminne* (victory of love).

Alder Woman.

This piece of oral tradition, preserved by minstrel poetry in 1221, displays a common theme of Celtic myth: the hero or king marries the goddess of the land. She might appear rough (like tree bark) in this world, but on other levels of reality she is of angelic splendour. The phases of madness in the Wildwood were initiation rites into other states of consciousness. The journey by ship finally symbolizes the transition into another dimension.

In Irish myth, the Alder appears twice; Diarmuid and Grania as well as Deirdre hide on their flight in the Alder swamps of Argyll, in Scotland. However, this teaches us no more about this tree than the *Averni* — the Gaulish Tribe of the Alder — of which we only have the name.

In Welsh myth, however, the Alder is the sacred tree of the mythical king, Bran the Blessed, whose name means crow or raven. In the Second Branch of the *Mabinogion* he appears as the rightful owner of the Cauldron of Rebirth, but later returns fatally wounded from a war with Ireland in which the cauldron was destroyed. Bran's death marks the end of an era, and the transition to the next is characterized by a mystical scenario: his fellows, the seven Welsh survivors of the war, follow Bran's instructions and cut off his head, which then talks and keeps them company for seven years, until one of the group accidentally breaks the spell. According to legend, the head of King Bran is buried at the Tower in London — hence the ravens there, according to legend, as a magical protection for Britain.

In Germany, the archetype of the Alder King became famous again through a ballad by Goethe published in 1782. Although believed to be based on a misinterpretation. Goethe found the term in Herder's *Volkslieder* (Folk Songs) from 1779, in which the Danish *ellerkonge* (elfin king) was mistranslated as Alder king (*eller* means Alder). However, the Alder King and Queen precede any of our present languages.

The Alder Woman was known before medieval times or even the Iron Age. The majority of prehistoric, anthropomorphic wooden figures found in various bogs of Britain and Ireland have either male or hermaphrodite forms. One alone is female, and is made from alder wood. It dates from between 728 and 524 BC and was found in a peat bog at Balachulish, on the west coast of Scotland, where it was sunk in a bog or lake, probably as an offering (Coles 1990, 316–20; 1998, 164–172).

Inspiration

Alder looks out for places of water; it lives with water, feeds on it, and co-operates with water. If you contemplate an Alder by a brook you might see that it not only shares the minerals from below, but also something else from above; particular frequencies of light are channelled downwards. Sunlight hits water directly, but sunlight through an Alder tree is a very different thing!

The tree simultaneously absorbs the flowing, cleansing and renewing qualities of the stream, and some of the life-giving water is taken up into the crown and spread over the land. Thus Alder is a medium, and under its canopy creates a microcosm, a refreshing, cool, shady space where fertility is nourished by water and celestial energies alike.

In linking Sun and water the Alder is related to the Ash, but Alder comes from the heart of the Earth. Ash's Greek name *klethra* is derived from *kleio* (to enclose, surround). It is a weaver of life and its tapestry is ever-changing.

The flames of Alder are green, but its blood is red. Alder is the bleeding mother and the wounded healer who understands; it is the listener, who can listen to your sorrow and weave your tears into her life-giving carpet. Master of the elements, Alder can heal with water, fire, earth and air. The weary will find strength in the lush realm around her; the depressed will find light in her aura, and warmth and comfort in the touch of her spiritual heart; and the angry will find peace. Emotional blockages will be washed away by the soft, floating qualities of tree and river if you are willing to let go. One might have to bleed like the Alder for a while, but she can help to heal one's wounds.

Willow

Willow family: *Salicaceae*
White Willow *(Salix alba)*

Physical appearance

Owing to the fact that Willow is a *genus* with over five hundred species, 'Willow' in this chapter refers specifically to the White Willow *(Salix alba)*.

The White Willow is recognizable from far away by its wide, round crown, which unfolds explosively on a trunk that often is slanted. Its floating form already shows its kinship with the water element.

Willow bark.

Willow. Sketch by Martin Klatt.

Accordingly, Willow enjoys well-ventilated, moist soil, preferably near stretches of water. Willow is waterproof and can tolerate long floods. The soil around the tree's flat root system may, however, be washed away by brooks. Trees blown over by the wind or storms, even fragments of trunks or branches, often just carry on growing in a modified direction. A horizontal trunk might create a whole thicket of new shoots. Single twigs can also take root in moist soil. This incredible regenerative power makes White Willow the ideal colonizer of river valleys, that are frequently exposed to spring floods. White Willow is not found at altitudes above 800 m (2,600 feet).

The members of the willow family not only share fast growth and soft, not very durable wood, but also the ability to create hybrids. In Europe as well as in North America, more than a dozen willow species are found. The White Willow has long, lance-shaped, pointed leaves, which are four to six times longer than they are wide. The Goat Willow *(Salix caprea)* — in England, also called the Pussy Willow or, in Ireland, the Sally Willow — with its broad elliptic leaves can usually endure dry conditions, being able to live on dumps, quarries, and wastelands or on the edges of moors. This species can be found in light mountain woodlands up to 2,000 m (6,550 feet).

It should not be confused with the American Pussy Willow *(Salix discolor)* which is yet another species.

Its ability to produce suckers and grow from cuttings makes the White Willow potentially immortal. The age of a single tree, however, is comparatively modest: White Willow, up to 25 m (80 feet) in height, hardly lives beyond 100 to 120 years. Goat Willow (6–10 m; 20–35 ft,) can reach more than five hundred years of age.

In the natural cycle willow wood soon falls prey to wood fungi. Willow reacts incredibly well to storm damage as well as pollarding (see pages 90f). Such rejuvenating measures spark off its will to live and joy to grow.

All willows are dioecious: the single trees are either male or female. The flowers appear early in March, (Goat Willow even earlier), and are an important bee food. The inflorescence is silky, grey-silver catkins, and the seeds are hairy; those of White Willow are silky-plumed to fly to new habitats. The seeds have a robust ability to germinate and grow.

Salix babylonica, the most widespread of the various weeping willows, was only brought from Asia a few centuries ago.

Healing

Willow bark is a time-honoured remedy — used by Hippocrates, Plinius, Paracelsus, Culpeper and others — and has been used for soothing pains, particularly rheumatic ones, and has febrifugal, sudorific, and astringent effects. The main active component is salicin, which oxidizes in the human body to become salicylic acid. Its discovery in 1827 led to the synthesis of acetylsalicylic acid in 1898, better known as the analgesic *aspirin*. Like aspirin, willow bark has one disadvantage: it irritates the stomach lining, and is not recommended any more. However, it can be used for gargling in case of bleeding gums or mouth inflammations, or as a footbath for sweaty feet. In the past willow bark was also used to treat inflammations of the digestive tract, kidney and bladder problems, rashes and headaches.

As a soother of rheumatic pain, Willow is a good example of the way nature offers the cure as a reflection of the affliction — here, wetlands.

As a Bach Flower Remedy, Willow *(Salix vitellina)* helps people who always blame circumstances or others for their misfortunes, to enhance their sense of personal responsibility and think constructively.

Tradition

Since the earliest time, Willows have been associated with the moon and female powers, particularly those of psychic ability and divination through
water, healing and magic. Graves, for example, mentions magic mists
being raised by 'willow spells' in ancient Greece. Thus, many ancient goddesses had their willows. The Sumerian goddess, Belili, ruled over the
Moon, love and the Underworld, and resided in willows, springs and
wells. In Greece, Persephone had a sacred grove 'remarkable for its black
poplars and aged willows,' to which Odysseus is sent by Circe to meet the
spirit of a dead seer (Graves 1975, 2.359). The Willow was sacred to poets,
the *wind in the willows* giving inspiration. Circe, the moon goddess and
daughter of the Sun god, Helios, also had a willow grove, dedicated to
Hecate, the goddess of death. The Greek name for willow was *helike*, and
Helike, the Willow, was the sister of Amalthea, the goat, who suckled Zeus
and Pan when they were babies. At Mount Helicon, named after Willow,
resided the nine muses, priestesses of the moon goddess (Graves 1970 1.189
& 1999, 168).

In the Christian era, the Willow was declared to be in league with Judas,
the devil and witches. The tree that wickerwork was made from became
wicked, evil. But despite widespread witch stories, country folk continued
to go to the Willow for relief of their ailments and diseases, drawing on its
power by means of folk medicine, spells and white magic.

Willows respond well to pollarding, and can be harvested annually or
biannually. Many types of willow were used to produce cradles and coffins,
wattle-and-daub walls, furniture, fences and all kinds of baskets, as well as
for food, storage, wood gathering, fishing and sowing. These ancient traditions fell largely into disuse during the twentieth century because of new
customs and materials such as plastic.

Another practical use for the Willow is harp making. The oldest and best-
preserved Celtic harp — the twelfth century Brian Boru harp from Ireland
— has a body carved from a single piece of willow wood, while the knee
and pillar are made of Oak. In this way the instrument unites male (see Oak)
and female in perfect balance.

An Irish legend from the *Milesian Cycle* associates the Willow with music
and psychic revelation. In this particular story, *Maon, Son of Ailill,* a young
man, knows the sad secret of King Labraidh and eventually the burden of
the secret makes him ill. A Druid is called to heal him and sends the youth
to a remote crossroads to reveal his secret to a tree. The tree is a willow.
Shortly after this the harpist, Craftiny, needs a new harp and unwittingly

Willow.

makes one from that very willow tree. Later, in the king's hall, to the amazement of all, the harp reveals the secret on its own and thereby brings healing to the kingdom.

In the Far East, soothsayers divined 'by the help of a number of willow rods, which they placed upon the ground, uttering their predictions as they gathered them up one by one' (Philpot 1994,102).

In Scotland, Willow was thought to represent strength and harmony. A peeled willow wand served the Lord of the Isles as a rod of justice. It was held for 'speaking justice as well as when they were initiated. This practice was continued by most major clan chiefs' (Fife 1994). In his book, *Warriors and Guardians,* Hugh Fife also speaks of different local 'rituals and customs that evoked the inner characteristics of the [Willow] tree.'

A Christian association of (Weeping) Willows with grief and sadness stems from Psalm 137: 'By the waters of Babylon, there we sat down and wept, when we remembered Zion. On the willows there we hung up our lyres.' However, The Lord ordered rejoicing at the Feast of Tabernacles with branches of willow, and nothing in the Willow itself justifies an association with grief. Instead, Willow is a tree of vitality and joy, and was one of the trees from which the Life Rod was taken. The old Ukrainian blessing for 'Willow Sunday' (Palm Sunday) states:

> Become big, like the Willow,
> And healthy, like the water,
> And rich, like the Earth
> (Mannhardt 1875, 257).

Inspiration

Interestingly, all objects traditionally made from willow are containers and vessels. Containers are for receiving which, in symbolic language, is the archetypal feminine quality. In the Celtic harp it is the hollow body which receives the vibration of the linear (male) string, allows it to resonate, and gives birth to something new: a rich sound that expands into the world.

Everywhere the Willow has been associated with the Moon and female powers. Willow is at one with the moon; it is a moonbeam, a drop of dew, a water nymph embodied in tree shape. As the Moon receives its light from the Sun and reflects it, so Willow prefers to stand and hang over water where it receives reflected light from below. Willow breathes with the magnetic tides of the Moon, and with the ebb and flow of the waters of the Earth. In this lies rhythm — and music.

Poplar

Willow family: *Salicaceae*
Black Poplar *(Populus nigra)*

Physical appearance

The Black Poplar is, after Alder and Willow, the third tree of the riverside meadows and boggy wetlands. It grows up to 30 m (100 feet) in height, and its thick trunk usually leans. The heavy branches grow in arching curves, forming a wide crown. From afar, it has one of the most characteristic tree shapes, and close up it displays a more rugged bark than any other tree. The foliage is light; the leaves, triangular or heart-shaped, move in the slightest breeze. The root system is far-reaching and stabilizing, and also drains the soil. Like Willow and Alder, the Black Poplar can live on floodplains, but it can also fertilize raw mineral soils, wastelands and deforested areas very quickly. Its crown and root systems are loose enough to allow undergrowth, while the decaying fallen leaves enhance the nitrogen concentration of the soil's upper layers.

Black Poplar is a large tree, naturally to be found in the valleys along the big streams. The Grey Poplar *(Populus x canescens)* is a hybrid of the latter and Aspen. The narrow Lombardy Poplar *(Populus nigra* cv. 'Italica'), cypress-like in appearance, is a form of Black Poplar and was introduced from Italy in the eighteenth century. It has been a common avenue tree in many parts of Europe ever since Napoleon started planting it along military roads in flat areas.

The quick growth of Poplars produces a soft, light wood, and elderly, solitary trees can easily become hollow. Despite their fast growth poplars can reach quite an age: the Black Poplar can reach about two hundred years; the White Poplar between three and four hundred years or more.

Poplars are best propagated from cuttings. The seeds of the Black Poplar are surrounded by white fluff for wind transportation, but they are rarely fertile since the tree is so rare — it is threatened with extinction in both England and Germany — and male and female trees often stand too far apart.

Poplar leaf.

Most of the tall, large-leaved poplars we see today on riverbanks are not Black Poplar, but hybrids between the European and the Canadian Black Poplar *(Populus x canadensis).*

Healing

Poplar's sticky buds contain high amounts of essential oil and resin, the positive effects of which have been known for centuries. As the tree drains the wetland, so it affects human metabolism, curing problems of the bladder, kidney and prostate, as well as rheumatism and gout. For tea, one to two teaspoons of the buds collected in early spring are used per cup, and two to three cups should be drunk daily. When applied externally the buds are helpful for burns, rashes, wounds, haemorrhoids and limb pains. The tea can be used for washing the skin, although the buds are best applied externally in the form of a cream. Young buds can also be added to spring salads.

Tradition

In the Middle Ages, the Black Poplar was quite common and the gentle curve of its trunk was often used as timber for cruck-framed buildings. As it is mostly inflammable it was also widely used for floorboards. Today, its

Black poplar.

slow-burning quality can still be found in matches. The fluff that surrounds the seeds was once used to stuff pillows and mattresses.

In Celtic and Germanic myth and legend, the Black Poplar hardly appears. This is partly due to the fact that poplars simply had not reached the West or the North — similarly there are none in Ireland. However, Frisians and Saxons must have come across the Black Poplar in their homelands, as well as the Celts in south and east England, but no lore has come down to us, and no old names for this tree, apart from the medieval *abele* for the White Poplar, exist. Most modern names are of more recent origin, being derived from the Latin *populus*, which in turn comes from the Greek, *pappalein* (to move).

Consequently, it is in Greek tradition that we find the only mentions. Leuke, a beautiful nymph, finally escapes the unwanted attentions of Hades, god of the underworld, by transforming herself into a Silver Poplar. She stands at the threshold to the underworld and is sacred to Persephone, the queen of the realm of the dead, who spends the summer above ground, and in winter retreats to the underworld with the vegetation. The Black Poplar, on the other hand, is sacred to Hecate, the death goddess (see also Aspen).

Inspiration

The ancient Greeks honoured poplars for their connection with the underworld, and planted them in graveyards. The Black Poplar, in particular, was sometimes approached with something close to fear because of its connection with the merciless Hecate. However, the goddesses of night and dark are originally aspects of the Moon, and it is not difficult to see the Silver and Black Poplar complementing each other as the full moon and new moon do. As a tree of the wetlands, the Poplar is naturally a tree of the Moon.

Whatever the names and meanings of the underworld deities, the myths identify the Poplar as a strong channel to other realms of consciousness — another gate. To understand more, one should visit it in its natural habitat.

In between the wide, flat horizons of flood meadows, wetlands or moorland the Poplar can be seen in its full glory. Its sap flows quickly, shifting huge amounts of water and, with the same vigour, it can take the observer on a journey that shifts his or her state of mind.

However, a second force can be seen at work in the Poplar's relationship with the wind, expressed by its almost continuously moving leaves, which make a sound like the distant sea, and by its tufted seeds which are entrusted to the wind. The wind is the domain of Mercury, the messenger of the gods, and the whispering of Poplar has always been considered prophetic, like that of its relative the Aspen.

Aspen

Willow family: *Salicaceae*
Aspen *(Populus tremula)*

Physical appearance

The Aspen is a definite light tree, which is found at the edges of woods. Owing to its ability to produce numerous suckers it is often found in a group. Aspen prefers loose clay or sand soils. Its modest claims on the soil are similar to those of Spruce, with which it often either shares mixed stands, particularly in North America, or periodically alternates. For example, Spruce pushes the Aspen out until a bark beetle epidemic, forest fire or storm create space again for the Aspen, which then loosens and vitalizes the soil. It can equally well give a new cover to raw ground, such as dumps or quarries, where it stabilizes and enhances the macrobiotic soil life, and attracts important fungi. After preparing the path for the mixed Wildwood, for example after an Ice Age, the flexible Aspen protects the edges of the wood from storm damage and sunburn.

The shape of the Aspen is slender and graceful, similar to Birch. Its bark, too, is bright, and green-grey to yellow-grey. The size of the tree varies with the soil quality: on sandy soils it is rather small, as in higher altitudes, up to 1,900 m (6,300 feet), but on the edge of fields it can easily reach 25 m (80 feet) or more. Aspen can lose branches in storms and quickly grow new ones. A single aspen tree rarely exceeds one hundred years of age.

Its leaves are particularly characteristic. In size they are between those of Birch and Black Poplar, but their shape is round, with blunt, toothed rims. The leaf stalks are extremely long and flexible, and are flat on both sides. This enables the leaves to quiver in even the slightest breeze — hence the saying: 'trembling like Aspen leaves.' This phenomenon is visually very attractive since the undersides of the rich green leaves are silvery. All Poplars use wind energy to enhance evaporation and thereby increase the amount of water and nutrients taken up from the soil.

Aspen.

Healing

All the effects and recipes described for Poplar also apply to Aspen. Apart from this, Aspen is one of the Bach Flower Remedies:

> The flower remedy increases inner strength and confidence, and helps to still fears and anxieties ... encouraging one into a wider range of experiences and adventures without fear holding one back (Scheffer 1990).

Aspen leaf.

Tradition

In Celtic tradition battle shields were made from this tree; its psychological shielding, increasing inner strength and confidence, might also have been the reason why Aspen was preferred to hardwoods for shields.

Furthermore, the living tree has always aided — for those who sought them — shifts of perception. In olden times the whispering of the Aspen leaves was deemed to be oracular, the messenger of the gods.

The veneration of this tree in pre-Christian times is comparable with that of Rowan, Elder and Yew. The priestly deeds of the Druids were connected with the Aspen and the trees were, therefore, wiped out by the onslaught of Christianity. In Norway, Austria, Germany, or even Celtic Scotland, these practices were replaced by a new image of a *hateful tree*. A book from 1777, reports that in Uist, Outer Hebrides: 'clods and stones and other missiles, as well as curses, are hurled at the aspen by the people' (Vickery 1995).

In ancient Greece, the tree was sacred to Heracles. According to myth, he wore an aspen wreath on a journey to the Underworld. The outside heat scorched the leaves dark, while their underside was bleached white by the sweat and radiance of the hero's forehead. Hence the Aspen was a sign of certainty that there is a return from the realm of the dead. The history of Aspen as an element of trust on the journey between the worlds goes back in time even further: Graves mentions golden crowns in the form of aspen leaves, which were found in Mesopotamian graves dating from 3000 BC. Later, the underworld link appeared again in old Ireland; the measuring tool of coffin makers was made of aspen wood.

It is therefore not surprising that the Church fought so fiercely against the Aspen: as the Church was trying to establish Christ as the only person who returned from the dead, any other tradition making similar claims had to be evil, including that of Aspen which, in the Middle Ages, was already more than four thousand years old.

Inspiration

The Aspen turns fear into opportunity. Its leaves enjoy the wind more than any other tree and are therefore a channel for the voice of Mercury, the messenger of more subtle spheres. An emblem of tolerance and flexibility, Aspen can receive impulses from all directions of the wind, and make them a harmonious part of its own movement and being. It continuously lives in the face of challenge and it does so with a smile and a light, graceful dance.

We do not need a remedy or ancient scriptures to experience this. Just position yourself opposite a group of Aspen trees for twenty minutes or so. Watch their glittering, enthusiastic light show, listen to the nuances of their whisperings and empty your mind. Then, if you wish, sit beneath the trees in complete silence, listen to their murmur and observe your inner impulses and sensations.

Hawthorn

Rose family: *Rosaceae*
Common Hawthorn *(Crataegus monogyna)*
Midland Hawthorn *(Crataegus laevigata)*

Physical appearance

Hawthorn is a one or multi-stemmed shrub or small tree, with three- or five-lobed leaves and short thorns. The gnarled bush appears sporadically in meadows, at the edges of woods and in light deciduous woodland. It is very hardy, with a deep root system which needs nutritious soil, preferably alkaline, but can also develop on rocky or clay soils. The Hawthorn unites deeply with the Earth. In pastures it can twist itself into impressive sculptures.

Hawthorn can often be found as part of hedgerows. A dense Hawthorn hedgerow — often mixed with Blackthorn, Elder, Hazel, Bramble and others — provides an ideal wind break, prevents the passage of cattle and protects open farmland; hence Hawthorn's ancient Germanic name *Hagedorn*, from *hegen* (to protect, care for, nourish). If not cut back, it can reach a height of 12 m (40 feet) and attain a considerable girth. Hawthorn can live for five hundred years or more.

Together with Blackthorn, this tree is one of the most important supporters of bird life. The berries provide food for many species, including blackbird, thrush, wood pigeon and robin, as well as small mammals such as voles and squirrels. Furthermore, the Hawthorn is very popular with nesting birds, which can also feast on the more than two hundred species of insects that experts have associated with it (Milner 1992).

Towards the end of May, after the unfolding of the leaves the flowers appear. Bisexual, white blossoms cover the dense bush, although the flowers are pink on some varieties. In late summer, the berries, the *haws*, turn from green to red. They contain one stone (pit) in the Common Hawthorn and two in the Midland Hawthorn.

Healing

Hawthorn strengthens the heart, balances the blood pressure and the heart's activity, and soothes cramps. It also relieves general fatigue and indifference, and serves as a relaxant for over-activity, but is mainly a remedy and tonic for the heart and circulation. The tea can be drunk for years, if necessary, without adverse side effects. One cup of boiling water is poured over two teaspoons of leaves, flowers or berries (which should be briefly pre-boiled), and left to infuse for ten minutes. A treatment involves two cups per day for at least three months. In homeopathy too, Hawthorn *(Crataegus)* is a valued heart tonic.

Freshly picked the leaves and fleshy, rather dry berries are a little-known tip for ramblers to curb hunger. The haws are nutritious and were eaten as part of the diet of early Neolithic man.

The berries can be prepared as a jam, and are delicious mixed with elderberries and apple. They can also be prepared as chutney. For chutney, 900 g (2 lb) of hawthorn berries and a teaspoon of salt are brought to the boil and simmered for one hour in half a litre of cider vinegar. The mixture is then sieved and the pulpy mixture boiled again with 350 g (12.25 oz) of brown sugar and one teaspoon each of ginger and nutmeg, together with some allspice, a few cloves and black pepper. Stirring constantly, heat the mixture slowly until it thickens, then pour into jars and seal.

Tradition

In many cultures Hawthorn has an uninterrupted history as the herald of spring and summer, and plays a central role in spring festivities, hence its other names May or May Tree. The themes involved are fertility, protection, marriage and bethrothal.

In Scottish myth and legend, the cuckoo (also a herald of spring) has a special affinity with the Hawthorn. In many places in Western Europe Hawthorn was present at May Day festivals and marriages, mainly because of its abundant white blossoms that were used for garlands, wreaths and other decorations, including those of the maypole.

The Romans placed Hawthorn twigs above the door to protect the house and stables from harmful spirits. In Christian times, various customs from Germany, Austria, France, England and Slav peoples valued this tree for its protective charms against evil, witches, vampires and lightning.

Hawthorn's main task, however, is to guard springs and wells. In Ireland, most sacred springs have a Hawthorn growing beside them. Many of these are decorated with colourful rags and the ground and stones beneath them are populated with little statues, lights and other gifts left in return for the *blessings* of the Hawthorn and the sacred spring.

According to an old local legend the *Glastonbury Thorn* sprang from the staff of Joseph of Arimathea who is said to have brought the Grail from the Holy Land to England. The staff is said to have taken root and developed into a fine hawthorn bush.

The oldest evidence of the spiritual power of this tree is a Hittite prayer written about 1500 BC (Hittite culture flourished during the second millennium BC in Anatolia, modern Turkey):

> You are the Hawthorn bush;
> In spring you clothe yourself
>   in white,
> At harvest time you dress in
>   blood red.
> You rip the fleeces of sheep
>   which pass beneath you.
> In the same way you pluck
>   any evil, impurity or
>   wrath of the gods
> from this initiate, who walks
>   through the gate [of your
>   hedge].   (Storl 1997)

Hawthorn bark.

Hawthorn.

More recently, the Hawthorn has been associated with the White Goddess, the archetype of female spring and fertility deities and muses. It was dedicated to Cardea, the Roman goddess of childbirth, who also protected infants. In Greek myth, Hera, Zeus' wife, conceived Ares (Mars in Roman tradition) and his twin sister, Eris, when she touched Hawthorn blossoms.

The tree's Icelandic name, *svefnthorn* (sleep thorn) reflects another notion. Odin used a hawthorn spine to send Brunhildeinto a magical sleep. In Brittany, Viviane put Merlin into and enchanted sleep under the Hawthorn until his reawakening in another age. In the fairy tale of Sleeping Beauty whose original German name is Dornröschen (Briar Rose), the princess pricks her finger on a spindle and sleeps for a hundred years in a castle covered with rose branches. Hawthorn belongs to the rose family; and spindles, like other small domestic items such as boxes, tool handles and cabinetwork, were traditionally made from the wood of this tree.

In the *Mabinogion*, Culhwych, nephew to King Arthur, has to fulfil thirty-nine (three times thirteen) tasks set by the giant Yspaddaden Pencawr (Giant Hawthorn), in order to marry his beautiful daughter, Olwen — 'She of the White Trace.' This reflects ancient rituals of tasks being set for bridegrooms and potential kings. Since Culhwych's tasks include finding the mystical Thirteen Treasures of Britain this story seems to have originally referred to his initiation into kingship, by marrying the goddess of the land who resides in the May tree.

Inspiration

It is noteworthy that during the magical sleep induced by Hawthorn the sleepers do not grow older. Merlin is as fresh as before when he returns, and so is Sleeping Beauty after a sleep of one hundred years. Similarly, Thomas the Rhymer from Scotland, who was lured to a magic hawthorn by the voice of a cuckoo, *sleeps* and visits fairyland in his trance, not ageing in common with fairyland visitors in other Celtic tales.

Is 'sleeping' only a euphemism for the protection that Hawthorn offers to those who journey to other dimensions while in its shelter? Communication with other realms is often a finely tuned act depending on a

Hawthorn leaves and berries.

delicate balance. Human activities in sanctuaries therefore require *protec-tion* from the multitude of chaotic influences from the outside, ordinary world. In sacred art, particularly in mandalas, the centre is often sur-rounded by invincible, castle-like walls or a circle of fire. In pre-historic Europe, consecrated hawthorn circles enclosed sanctuaries for ritual wor-ship (see Fife 1994).

Alchemists and herbalists characterized the celestial influences on Hawthorn as 'Venus in Aries,' suggesting a close intimacy between Venus and Mars, the planet which astrologically governs Aries. Mars is evident in the prickly thorns and the protection aspect. Venus, with her art, sexuality and beauty is evident in the shower of flowers and the blessings of the Hawthorn. Physically, these two could not be more intimately connected than in Hawthorn's bisexual flowers. Through the ages, the beauty of Venus in May has been celebrated more obviously, but the ultimate message of Hawthorn is unity, through the divine marriage of the male and female as-pects of the cosmic creative force.

Hawthorn.

Maple

Maple family: *Aceraceae*
Field Maple *(Acer campestre)*
Norway Maple *(Acer platanoides)*
Sycamore *(Acer pseudoplatanus)*

Physical appearance

The large family of maples, which incorporates Sycamore, are medium to very tall trees with a wide variety of leaf shapes. Often they have opposite, five- to seven-lobed leaves like the Sycamore. Maple inflorescence is often erect or spreading, and most species carry both genders in the same flowers. They are a good food source for bees. Maples are best known for their fruits, which are composed of two winged seeds. Air currents can spin them far afield. Their leaves also turn to the most amazing colours in the autumn. Maple leaves decay quickly and make excellent compost.

The Sycamore is a fast growing, huge tree, native to the mountains of central and southern Europe, but naturalized in north and west Europe. In the Alps it can be found up to altitudes of 1,600 m (5,250 feet). The bark of older trees breaks into irregular scales, which flake off like the bark of Plane trees, hence its Latin name, *pseudoplatanus*. Sycamores usually form beautiful round crowns, with a tendency to be slightly wider than they are high. They can grow to be hundreds of years old.

The Norway Maple *(Acer platanoides)* is originally a tree of northeast Europe, but with human help has spread all over south and west Europe, even reaching Ireland and North America. It is a tall tree but does not live long. Its leaves are extremely pointed; the Latin, *acer*, still bears the Indo-European root *ac, ak* (pointed, sharp).

The Field Maple *(Acer campestre)* — the only maple truly native to northwest Europe — is a slow-growing tree, and rarely grows higher than 10 m (33 feet). It is remarkable for the way it has softened the sharp points of the leaves to a more rounded form, with only three lobes accentuated. It grows as undergrowth in river valleys and light mixed woodlands, such as Ash

Sycamore leaves and seeds.   *An old Field Maple. >*

and Hazel, as well as in hedgerows. It is fond of warmth, light and rich soil (clay or chalk), which is strengthened and enhanced by its presence. Field Maple can reach two or even three hundred years of age. Its hard strong wood is valued even more highly than that of Sycamore, particularly for turning and carving.

Healing

Medieval medical tracts frequently mention Sycamore for its cooling and antiseptic effects. Preparations of bark and leaves were used for fever, swollen joints, inflamed eyes, insect bites or simply applied to tired feet. The young leaves can also be added to spring salads.

The most precious gift of Maple is its rich, sugary sap. The maple with the most abundant sap is the Sugar Maple *(Acer saccharum)*, which is widely grown in Canada. Other maples *bleed* as well but since the trees require proper treatment while being bled in spring, it is wiser to buy maple syrup than to experiment.

Tradition

No maple trees feature in European myth, though they were well known. The traditional Welsh art of carving love-spoons from sycamore wood was an early maple craft. Field Maple was the wood most often identified in the archaeological remains of Anglo-Saxon musical instruments, for example, in

harps. The tradition of using the wood of the Field Maple for musical instruments was particularly strong during the Renaissance and Baroque periods, and still continues today.

Inspiration

The first movement of every plant is vertical: the root moves downwards and the shoot upwards, following the light; the latter being the sphere of the Sun. Grasses and reeds are content with this, but most other higher plants also develop the urge to unfold horizontally, expanding into the surrounding space. Since ancient times the cosmic force guiding the horizontal expansion has been called *Jupiter*. In anthropocentric astrology, Jupiter denotes the principles of expansion, generosity and abundance, and its influence on the world of plants is similar. The physical planet, for its part, takes twelve times longer than the Earth to complete its orbit around the Sun; its influences on Earth are thereby in harmony with the Sun's influences (12 months, 12 years). The cosmic force balancing Jupiter is Saturn, which brings contraction, limitation and defined form. Together they create beauty.

Of course, these powers are modified by other forces, in a multitude of different ways, as it is reflected in the multitude of species on Earth. Mars and Venus, for example, alter the main shoot, and work on the reproductive organs. A unique mixture of impulses from the formative forces forms every species.

Maples are the trees that most clearly display the work of Jupiter. In various ways the Maple takes hold of the surrounding space, equally welcoming all of the directions.

— The branches in the younger parts of the crown fork time after time, creating more and more ends to touch the outside world.
— The inflorescence appears particularly at the outer areas of the crown, again orientated towards the outside.
— The leaves are wide and big. Unmistakably, they point to between five and seven directions of the compass, the eighth being the leaf stalk.
— The seeds are not in a hard shell and are winged. When these *propellers* glide through the air and spin, they point in every possible direction.

Thus the physical form of Maple reveals a positive openness to learn and receive from the universe. Maple is the archetypal antenna for impulses from the higher spheres. Therefore, its presence relaxes, cools, soothes and balances. It helps us to clear the head, and at the same time helps to harmonizes our thinking.

Elm

Elm family: *Ulmaceae*
Wych Elm *(Ulmus glabra)*
English Elm *(Ulmus procera)*

Physical appearance

Elms are large deciduous trees that can reach 40 m (130 feet) in height. The alternating leaves are elliptical and pointed, and have, depending on the subspecies, between seven and nineteen pairs of veins. The doubly toothed margins and clearly asymmetrical bases are striking characteristics of the leaves. On Wych Elm *(Ulmus glabra)* the leaves are bristly. The leaves of English Elm *(Ulmus procera)* — a variety of the Field or Small-leaved Elm *(Ulmus minor)* — are usually smaller than those of Wych Elm. The European White Elm *(Ulmus laevis)* has a fringe of hairs on its papery seed wing. Most Elms live for five to six hundred years or more.

Wych Elm has fine twigs while the bark on its trunk is thick and rough with long, deep furrows. The overall shape of mature trees is slightly irregular and open, like Poplar, although Elm creates dense foliage. Thus Elm combines the characteristics of softwood species (such as Poplar) with those of hardwood species (such as Beech).

The appearance of the bisexual flowers in early spring gives the whole, leafless crown a reddish tinge. The winged seeds ripen quickly and fall in June.

Elms prefer stands in fertile river valleys (Small-leaved Elm) or, at higher altitudes, near small mountain streams (Wych Elm). It is noteworthy that in the northern parts of central Europe Field Elm no longer reproduces by seed but almost exclusively by suckers, which arise from the root system. As a result Field Elm can colonize places where thick ground cover, owing to rich soil, can suffocate tree seedlings.

Elm.

Dutch Elm Disease

Tragically the twentieth century witnessed a massive worldwide decline of the elm population. Dutch Elm Disease in its present form first appeared in northwest Europe around 1919. It died down in the 1940s after causing the loss of between ten and forty per cent of elms in various European countries. In the late 1960s, a second and far more destructive outbreak occurred which reached its peak in the 1990s, killed the majority of mature elms. The disease is still spreading in parts of Scotland and Ireland, as well as in Canada, Asia and New Zealand.

Research has shown that while the fungus *Ophiostoma ulmi* caused the first pandemic, the second is from a slightly different species, *Ophiostoma novo-ulmi*. Like its predecessor, this highly aggressive pathogen is spread by the elm bark beetle *(Scolytus)*. Before their final chrysalis stage, the beetles attack the forks of the younger elm branches and infect the tree with the fungus. The fungus produces a wilt toxin *cerato-ulmin*, which fatally disturbs the water balance of the tree, resulting in the wilting of entire branches. A tree infected in the spring can die in the same year.

The beetle only attacks mature trees, and millions of suckers can appear

Elm bark.

after the old trees have died. However, on gaining a height of 3–12 m (10–40 feet) the tree's bark becomes attractive to the beetle. Thus new elm generations are quickly followed by new outbreaks of the pathogen. Despite enormous numbers of small and semi-mature trees the population of mature elms is very low. A few old elms, however, have survived, particularly Wych Elms that seem to cope better with infections.

The spread of the fungus has been studied carefully over the decades, but its origin remains a mystery. In 1996, in *New Horizons in Dutch Elm Disease Control*, Professor C. Brasier, from the Forestry Commission in Edinburgh, wrote:

> The evolutionary and geographical origins of *Ophiostoma ulmi* and of the two races [the American and the European] of *Ophiostoma novo-ulmi* remain unknown.

In 1993, a third Dutch elm disease fungus, *Ophiostoma himal-ulmi*, was found in the Western Indian Himalayas. It is also spread by the elm bark beetle which breeds in the local Himalayan Elm *(Ulmus wallichiana)* but does not cause problems: 'no wilt disease was seen on elms in the Himalayas' (Brasier 1996, 24).

Various forestry commissions worldwide have tried different approaches to save and re-establish elms. In North America, various measures are combined, including the use of fungicides. In Great Britain, cutting out affected branches and the quick removal of dead trees is the favoured method. Scientists and authorities are, however, also looking into more far-reaching courses of action. In 1983, studies revealed that the fungus itself suffers from a disease, which has virus-like agents located in the fungus' cytoplasm. These were called the *d-factor*. Scientists are therefore attempting to attack the pathogen by releasing beetles carrying fungi weakened by genetically chosen d-factors. Secondly, they are using genetic engineering, introducing anti-fungal genes to the elms. Professor Brasier called the English Elm 'an excellent model system for genetic manipulation of broadleaved trees,' but he is also concerned about the 'risk of "escape" of novel DNA beyond the engineered elm plants,' and the likelihood of disruption to *friendly* fungal or insect populations.

Healing

Elm bark is a time-honoured remedy for the skin. Dioscorides in the first century AD, knew its astringent, wound healing properties, and applied it to chronic rashes, abscesses and boils. Internally, Elm's diuretic, sudorific and blood-cleansing qualities were used to cure diarrhoea, internal bleeding and fever, and to soothe gout and rheumatism. Responding to the present ecological situation, however, elm bark should be left alone, although if you find a mature elm tree with seeds, you could roast them and sprinkle them over a salad or a soup.

In Bach Flower Therapy Elm *(Ulmus procera)* touches on the principle of responsibility. When people who normally manage well suddenly feel overwhelmed, exhausted and doubtful the remedy restores their confidence, and their ability to put problems in perspective.

Tradition

Elm has always been a highly thought of tree. According to the *Eddas*, the first human couple was created from two pieces of wood; the man from ash, the woman from elm. At least it is commonly supposed that the woman's name, *Embla*, is derived from the Old Norse, *álmr* (elm).

In Nordic tradition elm was a particularly important guardian tree, even in nineteenth century Sweden it was still a *Varträd*, a 'guardian tree' of the farm. In old France, justice was declared under elms and meetings held. At Gisors, on the border of Normandy, there was a mighty Elm beneath which the kings of France and dukes of Normandy held conferences, as the tree was big enough to shelter both their retinues. It was cut down later by order of King Philippe Auguste who wanted to break with the Plantagenet dynasty. He was not the only one who felt threatened by the powerful presence of old Elm trees and the common respect they engendered. Various laws tried to contain the ancient worship at elm and other trees. The tenth century Christian Saxon king, Edgar, wrote:

> We decree that every priest shall anxiously advance Christianity, and forbid tree worship, divination with the dead, omens, charms with songs, and many other illusions which are practised in asylums on elms, and on various other trees, by which many are perverted who ought not be so. (Heath 1912)

Things gradually changed, but for about three hundred years an elm tree at Richmond, Surrey, was known as *the Queen's Elm*, 'planted by Queen Elizabeth [I] herself' (Folkard 1892, 324). Unfortunately we do not know her reasons for planting it. In many areas elm trees were important in agriculture, whether as cattle fodder or to define the times for sowing.

The ancient Greeks and Romans planted elms at burial places, and similar evidence can be found much later, in the west of Europe. In England, elm was the traditional wood for coffins.

In Greek myth the three sisters, known as the Hesperides, who guarded the Golden Apples fetched by Heracles, were transformed at their death into a willow, a poplar and an elm tree. In the legend of Orpheus, the hero mourned the death of his beloved Eurydice, and from the sound of his lyre an elm grove sprang up around him. When he returned from Hades, he rested under an elm tree, and all the plants and animals of the wood crowded peacefully around him, enchanted by his music.

Inspiration

Elm always appears in the middle. Physically, it combines characteristics of soft and hardwood trees; it heals our skin, which is the medium between the outside and the inside; as well as the digestive tract, which internally transforms physical impressions from outside. Spiritually, Elm mediates between the living and the dead, seen through Elm's connection with burial practices; between humans and nature spirits, as one of the *Varträd* in Scandinavia; while in both England and Germany, the folk name *elven* or *Elfenholz* (elfin wood) is also used for the tree.

Even more than Poplar or Aspen, Elm is governed by Mercury who is the archetype of communication and information exchange. Even the practical uses of its wood — for cart and wagon wheels, ships, coffins and water pipes — are all connected with transport, an area characteristically presided over by Mercury. Indeed the Elm is aligned with the planet Mercury, as indicated by the research of Lawrence Edwards (see Chapter 5).

If we are willing to consider that everything in the physical world reflects processes in the soul, we can see that the current, physical decline of Elm parallels the decline of mankind's readiness to communicate with other realms — ancestors, nature spirits, and the plant and animal kingdoms.

Injecting fungicides or engineered genes might cure the symptoms of Dutch elm disease but not the cause. If you have an elm in your garden you can try a gardeners' trick from Canada: Elder has an odour that many insects find disagreeable and can be planted next to Elm.

Beech

Beech family: *Fagaceae*
Common Beech *(Fagus sylvatica)*

Physical appearance

Over wide areas of middle Europe, Beech is the natural dominating deciduous tree. This is because Beech knows best how to use light. However, it
does need the protection of the forest, as young plants are threatened by
frost and draught. Old trees are light sensitive because in direct sunlight
their smooth bark does not protect well against overheating. When trees on
shady stands are suddenly exposed to sunlight their bark is often burned
since it cannot adapt quickly enough to the increase in radiation.

Beech forms dense woods, creating vast pure or mixed Beech woods
(mostly with Oak or Spruce). Beech dominates its stand to such a degree
that other plants can hardly exist, apart from some herbs which blossom before the beech foliage closes over, or shady trees like Holly, Spruce or Yew.
Otherwise, the spacious, high halls of the beech wood belong exclusively to

*The washed-
out roots of the
beeches on the
mound at
Avebury.*

the Spirit of Beech — its silver-grey columns, light playing in the green citadels high above, and a copper-coloured carpet of shed foliage.

Beech is only successful on its favoured stands, and requires fairly constant temperature and moisture conditions. It prefers soils rich in nutrients and moisture but can adapt to poorer limestone and dry chalk. Extreme conditions like flood plains, moorland, bogs, sandy soils and mountains are happily left to others. On ground that is too boggy Beech runs the risk of being blown over by the wind since its root system does not penetrate deeply. Beech loves the mild but cool and moist climate of western central Europe — Beech needs at least 650 mm (26 inches) of rain a year. Its specific needs are probably the reason why it returned so slowly after the Ice Age. It was spread over England more by man during the last two, than on its own during the previous six millennia. On the European Continent its numbers were rather reduced by man, to the advantage of Spruce forests.

Beech gives structure to the soil by draining, ventilating and strengthening it. The tree creates a brittle, but mild, humus that tends to be slightly acidic.

The wood of Beech is heavy and hard, revealing something of the tree's persistence and patience. The Beech tree is an icon of strength and firmness, but its wood is not durable: the absence of tannic acid or resin, as in Oak and conifers respectively, make it prone to early decay. Beech trees can reach between two hundred and fifty to three hundred years of age, in rare single cases even five hundred years, but they often fall prey to core rot during their second century.

According to local conditions Beech starts flowering after 30–60 years. A single tree carries both sexes. Two or three fruits, the beechnuts, sit together in a woody shell covered with soft spikes, and fall noisily in the autumn. Beech produces an incredible amount of seeds, particularly in 'mast years' (years when trees are particularly laden with fruit and seeds), which is why, for centuries, Beech and Oak were the two most important trees for feeding livestock, especially pigs.

The Copper Beech *(Fagus purpurea)* with its deep purple leaves is a variety of the Common Beech.

Healing

Beech bark, wood, leaves and seeds are used for their astringent, antiseptic and disinfecting properties. Beech is generally cooling: a bark preparation is an old remedy against fever, and merely being under beech trees cools the head, gives clarity, refreshes and stimulates.

Beech wood ash was once used in ointments for sores and boils, for both animals and humans. If one soaks the ash overnight in warm water and drains it the following morning, the result is *beech leach*, a soapy solution, rich in potassium, which was used for washing and scrubbing.

Like the leaves of many deciduous trees Beech leaves can be eaten on their own, but are much nicer in salads and soups. The cooling and anti-septic tea of the leaves can be used in compresses to cure sties, or for wash-ing slightly inflamed skin.

Beechnuts are very rich in protein and contain up to fifty per cent fatty oil. After peeling they can be roasted for salads or muesli. The oil can be ex-tracted by pressing and is especially tasty for frying fish; this cooking oil was much better known in the past than it is today.

The Bach Flower Remedy of Beech enhances sympathy and tolerance. It balances narrow-minded, hard, rigid and intolerant states, where one is self-righteously locked into one's own inner space, judging but not understand-ing others.

Tradition

Beech has always been an important tree in the life of humans, as can be seen by its Roman and Greek names which are derived from the Greek and Latin *phagein* and *fagus* respectively, which both stem from words meaning 'to eat.' Together with Oak and Sweet Chestnut, and other members of the beech family, it was one of the main providers of food for man and beast. No myths survive, however, which reflect this fact. Beech does not appear in the Irish tree alphabet, simply because it did not grow in Ireland at that time. It was abundant under Anglo-Saxon and Germanic skies, but people did not write about it, but *on* it. The tree's association with writing and runes was so strong in the age of dawning literacy that it outshone even the connection with the Oak, which provided gall apples for the ink of early manuscripts. The first books were made of small beech boards, as an alternative to scrolls, hence the relationship of the words for beech and book. For example, Anglo-Saxon: *bok* (beech) and *bec* (book); modern German: *Buche* (beech) and *Buch* (book); Swedish: *bok* (beech) and *bok* (book); Old High German: *buohha* (beech), *buoh* (book), *buohhin* (made of beech wood).

The German word for letter, *Buchstabe* (beech stick), suggests that this wood was widely used for rune practice, although there is no archaeologi-cal evidence for this as beech wood decays so quickly. However, Beech is

Beechwood. Watercolour by Maxine Relton.

Beech tree at Seven Leazes.

Beech. >

linked to scripture, writing and the preservation of the word, which has survived over time.

Beech's relationship with the Greek *phagein* (to eat) is no accident either;
in Aramaic, too, the same word denotes 'daily bread' and 'understanding.'

Inspiration

Beech, to a high degree is the embodiment of the influences of Saturn — not
many trees, apart from Birch, Maple and Sycamore, bear the marks of a
planet so clearly. Saturn is the force that 'isolates a being from the surroundings, individualizes it, so that it can develop an inner rhythm in itself
and through itself' (Steiner 1993). Under the influence of Saturn, a tree like
Beech tends to create its own space It reveals the Saturnian principles of
contraction, compression and isolation in many ways.

— The tall trunk dominates the tree. The arrangement of branches is more
   affected by their relationship to the trunk than to the tree's surroundings.
— Slow growth and dense wood.
— The outer bark does not split as in other trees, but expands with the trunk
   throughout the life of the tree. Thus it protects the trunk from the outer
   world.
— The leaves are very small for such a vital tree. The leaf stalks are very
   short and the leaves have smooth margins.
— The woody, spiky fruit capsules isolate the seeds from their surroundings.
— The Beech wood as a whole creates its own, shady, isolated world. A solitary tree acts accordingly: the alpha-shape of Beech is a closed, almost
   perfect half-sphere.
— The corresponding rhythms of Beech and Saturn have already been discussed (see Planets and Trees). Beech only starts reproduction after one
   or two revolutions of Saturn.

The spiritual gift offered by Beech is to find one's own centre, and to be
centred; to be in no hurry; to make careful and clear decisions; and to move
decisively in one's chosen direction.

Its other features are typical of Saturn: the cooling, astringent, medicinal
effects; its links with writing (Saturn is also known as *the preserver*); and the
effects of the Bach Flowers, which destroy isolation, but at the same time refresh the abilities of discipline and perseverance.

Oak

Beech family: *Fagaceae*
Pedunculate Oak *(Quercus robur)*
Sessile Oak *(Quercus petraea)*

Physical appearance

In spring, the Pedunculate Oak is one of the last trees to have leaves, to avoid late frosts. It is sensitive to hard winter frosts, an attribute that hinders its distribution in the far north and in Siberia. Soils in which its roots cannot be fully deployed are often lost to its close relative, Beech. However, Oak can tolerate soils that are quite dry or quite moist, hence its dominance in England, and it has effective helpers for spreading its seeds: squirrels and jays bury acorns as food provisions. The acorns are such a rich food deposit for seedlings that they can even come up in shade or dense grass.

Oak is the most motherly, or fatherly, tree of the temperate climate, considering the multitude of species living in its close vicinity. More than five hundred species of spiders and insects rely on Oak, as well as a wide variety of birds and animals. The nutritious acorns of some Oak species comprise about seventy per cent starch and sugar, and six per cent protein. However, in all Oaks, the acorns ripen in open cups, while the fruits of the other members of the beech family (Beech, Sweet Chestnut) grow in closed and spiky containers. The acorns of Pedunculate Oak sit on long stalks, while the leaves are nearly stalkless, Sessile Oak behaves exactly the other way round. Oaks are wind-pollinated and carry both sexes on one tree.

The Pedunculate Oak has a vast root system, and a tendency to develop a thick trunk that supports its powerful metabolism. Thick bark protects the tree from heat, and even facilitates its survival in forest fires, although oaks are struck by lightning more often than most other trees, probably because they grow above subterranean watercourses, and because they possess strong electrical currents.

Oak branches tend to sudden changes of direction and the irregular crown has an open shape, like the irregularly lobed leaves. The overall

Old Sessile Oaks in the unique ecology of Wistman's Wood, Dartmoor, England

shape is often wider than it is high; slender trees only develop in closely populated stands. Oak has firm and durable wood that has always been highly valued. Certain oaks have become famous by their impressive longevity — one thousand years and more — although most die after six to eight hundred years of age.

> The Monarch Oak, the Patriarch of trees,
> Shoots rise up and spread by slow degrees;
> Three centuries he grows, and three he stays
> Supreme in state, and in three more decays.
> (English saying)

Old Oak.

Healing

A high concentration of tannic acid makes oak bark very astringent, which is why it is used for tanning leather. It also has antiseptic, constipating and sterilizing properties. In older times, the tea of bark or leaves was used internally against diarrhoea, infections of the digestive tract, liver and bladder problems and bleeding. Externally, it was used in gargles, washes and hip-baths, and for treating rashes, wounds, burns, haemorrhoids, bleeding gums and swollen tonsils.

In hard times, acorns were not only eaten by animals but also by people. The main problem is to lessen their bitter taste. The best way is to cut the peeled acorns into small pieces and soak them in water. For a few days the water has to be changed regularly until it is of a light colour. Then, the acorns can be dried or roasted, and ground into flour. For baking bread, acorn flour is added to wheat flour, contributing an aromatic, nutty and, hopefully, not too bitter, taste. Roasted and ground acorns can also make a tasty coffee (one teaspoon per cup, can be mixed with cinnamon, dandelion root, etc.).

A homeopathic tincture, *Quercus,* is made from acorns and helps with problems of the liver and particularly the spleen.

As a Bach Flower Remedy, Oak relates to strength and endurance. It is for people who take their tremendous will power and devotion to duty too far,

Oak leaves.

thinking only of work and achievement, and who do not allow themselves to be at least partially guided. Oak teaches them to re-evaluate the playful, tender and trusting moments.

Tradition

The Oak has a long tradition as the king of trees. In the times of the ancient Greeks, the deva of the Oak grove of Dodona became the chief deity, Zeus. The Sacred Oak at Dodona was, like that of Delphi, a major oracle of the Old World, and an international place of pilgrimage for about one thousand years. Oak was also the sacred tree of Zeus' Roman equivalent, Jupiter, making it a prominent tree in Roman sacred groves.

German place names like *Dreieich* (Three Oaks) are believed to indicate ancient Germanic sanctuaries or *thing* places (gathering places for Germanic tribes or villages, for democratic discussion or justice). It is assumed that oak trees were also present in Druid groves because of the importance of Oak in Western Europe. The only evidence for Oak worship, however, comes from Gaul. Pliny reported a ritual of cutting the sacred mistletoe at a certain time of year, from an Oak tree.

In the Celtic harp of the Old Irish king, Brian Boru, Oak resembles the male creative aspect (see also Willow). Oak was sacred to all sky and thunder gods: Zeus, Thor and the Celtic, Taranis, as well as to Earth deities, as the Oak fed so many, particularly pigs which were sacred to mother goddesses such as Ceridwen. The Celtic name of Oak is related to 'tree' and 'door,' and the Welsh Bardic poem, *The Battle of Trees* (*Câd Goddau*), describes Oak as a door between the worlds:

> Before him tremble heaven and earth, Stout doorkeeper against the foe, is his name in all lands (117–120).

Even in the Christian age, Oak maintained much of its prestige, although, mainly for its material value. In many Christian countries Oak was the Yule Log for the mid-winter fire, and the door between the years. In other places, solitary trees in farmer's meadows were untouchable, not even fallen twigs were allowed to be removed, a custom that persisted even in recent centuries. The Church finally gave in and superimposed saints upon them, particularly Mary. In Germany, a good number of *Oaks of Mary* still exist in Bavaria.

In the Old Testament, most of the sacred trees that appear are called 'Oak,' even if they were of completely different species; for example, the Oak of Mamre, the Oak of Deborah.

Heroes like Robin Hood are eagerly identified with this tree, and every European country is invariably proud of *their* Oak. European economics since the Middle Ages were built on the wealth of wood, particularly Oak. In the seventeenth and eighteenth centuries, the English spoke of their oak ships as their 'wooden walls' and said that the 'heart of oak were our men' (Wilkinson 1981, 34f).

Merlin's Oak still exists today (as a stump) in his birth town of Carmarthen, Wales, and King Arthur's Round Table is believed, by many, to have been made of a single piece of Oak.

Inspiration

Despite being dedicated to Zeus and therefore Jupiter, Oak's astronomical relationship with Mars remains unaffected (see Chapter 5). In the plant world, Mars generally influences the development of the main shoot, either stimulating or inhibiting it. In its relationship to the Earth, Mars is the planet with the greatest dynamic. When it is *behind* the Sun its distance from Earth is about seven times bigger than when, 390 days later, Earth and Mars are located on the same side of the Sun. However, then Mars stands opposite the Sun from the perspective of the Earth, and thus counterbalances the forces of the Sun. In this phase, Mars stimulates root growth.

Then, the planet ventures out again, far into space, and in conjunction with the Sun pulls the plant upwards. These influences are modified for all plants by other forces, but Oak embodies them with unusual clarity. They appear in:

— the rhythmical stimulation and inhibition of the shoots, resulting in the typical eccentric zigzag growth of the tree;
— the extraordinarily strong tap root;
— the unusually accentuated development of single branches at the expense of an even, harmonious crown;
— the stout shape which is a result of inhibited force, just as the dense, firm wood is;
— the lobes and indentations of the leaf shape, which also reflect this rhythm.

This oak at the forest's edge is an impressive guardian. Painting by Martin Klatt.

Various species of Oak modify these influences, which can be seen by the multitude of leaf, and tree, shapes. The leaves of the Holm Oak (*Quercus ilex*), an evergreen native of the Mediterranean, have no indentations and are smooth-edged and oblong. The whole tree has a much softer impression.

Investigations into electrical currents in trees (see Chapter 3) have shown that Oak is a very special tree. Its vitality is far higher than that of any other tree in the same climate (only Birch is close, although birches can charge more in light, and are much smaller). Oak pushes into existence with tremendous force. With its unique, huge tap root it stands in the earth like a spear rammed in by the gods, and brings some of this primeval creative energy to the ground, infusing the groundwater with it and distributing it all over the land and among all its inhabitants.

The Spirit of Oak takes us into the world, not in the birth phase as Birch does, but in the prime of life. This is reflected by its numerous gifts to humankind: wood for trading and war ships, houses, barrels, tables, doors, fuel and bark for tanning.

As well as its rhythmic connection with the planet Mars, Oak associates with the astrological side of Mars, which represents creative male energy. In the past, Mars was not simply a war god, as many people think today:

> The Celtic Mars possessed, above all, a protective or guardianship role, and he was frequently associated with healing cults in Central Europe' (Green 1992, 162).

Oak in Celtic sources is sometimes called *the tree of the warrior,* but it gives power to anyone who goes there. While other trees emanate more specialized qualities, Oak brings raw life energy and inspiration. Its neutrality can be used for war or peace, healing, courage and inner strength alike.

Holly

Holly family: *Aquifoliaceae*
Holly *(Ilex aquifolium)*

Physical appearance

Holly is the only evergreen, *leafy* tree of northwest Europe. In central Europe, however, it remains more like a shrub. Its shiny, leathery, waxy leaves are very striking, and have wavy and spiny margins. The accentuated spines of the leaves are sharply pointed but these become less spiky towards the higher part of the crown, where animals cannot reach. Holly needs the protection of the tall forest from the cold. It is also not resistant to hard winter frosts and consequently, does not venture into Eastern Europe.

Holly thrives in wooded pastures or open deciduous woods, preferably Oak, and is the only tree that can survive in the shade of Beech woods. It grows patiently and has great staying power. Correspondingly, its high-quality wood is of an even texture; hard, tough and heavy. Holly grows on sandy, slightly acidic or lime soils. Holly trees can reach two hundred and fifty to three hundred years of age.

When about twenty years of age Holly starts to flower. Small, white, finely scented blossoms appear in May and June from the leaf nodes. The tree is usually dioecious (separate male and female trees) but where the distribution is too sparse for insect fertilization, Holly ensures local continuance of the species by producing both genders of flower on the same tree. The berries, at first green becoming bright red in the autumn, remain on the tree all winter, and are an important food for birds. Holly seeds only germinate in the second or third year.

Healing

The berries are poisonous for humans, and are highly emetic and laxative. The leaves, however, are known for their healing properties. Tea can be made from one or two teaspoons of chopped leaves soaked overnight in one cup of water, and brought briefly to the boil in the morning. One or two cups can be drunk in single sips during the day. The tea is used for curing feverish colds, cooling fever, soothing coughs and loosening mucus.

The Bach Flower remedy relates to all-encompassing love. It is for those who have disconnected themselves and have feelings of jealousy, envy or hatred, or do not feel anything anymore. Holly opens the heart.

Tradition

Owing to its prickly leaves, four-lobed flowers (mirroring the four points of the cross) and blood red berries, Holly has been frequently associated with Christ. According to central European tales, the palm fronds in Jerusalem became spiky when the crowds changed from cheering Jesus to condemning him. The Church normally used such ideas to condemn a plant, but instead Holly became an important plant for Church decorations, hence its modern German name, *Stechpalme* (stinging palm), which mirrors the Bible when God ordered Easter to be celebrated with *palm* leaves (Lev. 23:40). Holly's Latin name stems from *ilex* (evergreen) and *aquifolium* (needle-leaved).

Not everyone in Christian society was happy with the common acceptance of this plant, but many attempts against it failed, meeting fierce opposition from the common people. An English medieval ballad defends the Holly traditions, which are still an intrinsic part of Christmas decoration: 'Who so ever ageynst Holly do crye, In a lepe shall he hang full hie. Alleluia!' (Folkard 1892, 377).

Holly does not appear much in sources of pre-Christian traditions, apart from documents containing the magic spells of the Anglo-Saxon herbalist shaman-doctors. One manuscript, for example, describes a stomach cure made by boiling chopped holly leaves in milk until tender, and then eating three pieces in the morning, and three in the evening, all after food (the number three was a sacred number to the Anglo-Saxons). The Anglo-Saxon word for Holly is *holegn*, clearly related to 'holy.'

Some traditions have Oak as the king of the *waxing* half of the year, when the days grow longer, and Holly as the king of the *waning* half.

A widespread country belief in the British Isles of unknown origin still regards Holly as the embodiment of the male forces of nature and Ivy as the female. When cutting hedgerows many people, particularly in Wales, will not touch any of the holly trees.

Holly leaves.

Inspiration

References to the Holly king can be traced back to about the twelfth century. Since the Anglo-Saxons' conversion to Christianity only began in the ninth century we might assume that the Holly king has pre-Christian roots. Even if oral traditions had been broken, holly re-emerges within the people.

Holly projects a remarkable sense of strength and clarity, a dignified form of decisiveness that comes from a vivid balance of head and heart. The Bach Flower remedy then is no surprise: unconditional love. Christian esoterics see the Crucifixion as the physical representation of divine love. In this sense, Holly's origins seem to link back to Christ, which perhaps explains why the Anglo-Saxons called it the 'holy' tree.

Hazel

Birch family: *Betulaceae*
Hazel *(Coryllus avellana)*

Physical appearance

Hazel is usually multi-stemmed and shrub-like, and forms half-spheres or umbrellas. The soft green leaves have fine doubly toothed edges and are clearly veined. After nine years a hazel starts to flower, and then does so every spring before its leaves unfold. The yellow, pliant male catkins appear around February. About a month later, the female flowers follow on the same tree, revealing fine crimson stigmas. Hazel does not self-pollinate. The nourishing nuts, rather small in the wild varieties, have white kernels enclosed in hard shells that often hang in bundles and are enveloped in leafy, ragged cups.

Hazel likes fertile soil, but was one of the first trees to populate the post-glacial tundra; it loves warmth, but it also resists extreme weathers. The spread of hazel populations often paralleled that of human settlement.

After the Ice Age, Hazel woods were dominant in Europe until other species succeeded. Hazel is intolerant of shade, and when shaded by others it may linger on for years but hardly flower. It thrives in light, mixed, deciduous woodland, for example, with Ash and Maple.

It is hard to tell the age of a hazel tree. Stems die after thirty to fifty years, but are replaced by an abundance of new shoots. In this way it looks forever young, while the actual plant, root or stump can be hundreds of years old.

Healing

Remains of hazelnuts have been found in the remains of human settlements from Neolithic times onwards. They always have been an important food for people in the north. The nutritious nuts contain vitamins A, B and C, as well as potassium, calcium, phosphorous, magnesium, iron, protein and

Hazel trees.

sixty to seventy per cent fatty oil. Hazelnuts can be eaten raw or roasted, and appear in countless recipes.

Leaves and bark are old remedies because they are astringent, staunch blood flow, are febrifugal and counteract the dilation of the blood vessels.

Tradition

Hazel was an ancient, widespread symbol of fertility, and was used in fertility rites, and later, in love and marriage ceremonies, from ancient times right through the early Christian era. Furthermore, Hazel was one of the trees (together with Rowan and Willow) which supplied the Life Rod. An even longer unbroken line of history exists for divination — a method for finding subterranean water supplies. Not only did the ancient Etruscans and Chinese use Hazel rods for this purpose thousands of years ago, but they are also still in use today.

Hazel has a very important role in Celtic mythology. In Ireland, nine hazel trees surround the source of all wisdom, known as Connla's Well, or the Well of Segais. From this 'true spring' emanate seven streams and 'over the well of the mighty waters stands the poets' music-haunted hazel' (Gwynn III 1913, 287).

> The nine hazels of Crimall the sage
> Drop their fruits yonder under the well:
> They stand by the power of magic spells
> Under a darksome mist of wizardry.
> (Gwynn III 1913, 293).

Salmon in the stream below eat the falling hazelnuts and thus absorb the wisdom contained therein. Fionn, the pupil of a master Druid, burns himself while preparing such a 'salmon of wisdom.' He sucks his burnt thumb and with it a drop of the cooking juice, and at that very moment he acquires the gift of prophecy. The *Hazel of Wisdom* is a source of Bardic inspiration. Scotland's Gallic name, *Caledonia*, is derived from the *Cal Dun* (Hill of Hazel), as does the Gallic term for wisdom, *cnocach*, which stems from the word for hazelnut, *cno*.

In Welsh myth, Arthur and his companions search for the mysterious Mabon ap Modron, the Son of the Great Mother, who disappeared without trace three days after his birth. No living being in the land knows his whereabouts, and finally the oldest animal in the land, the Eagle of Gwernabwy, sends them to the magic salmon, which is even older than the eagle. The salmon takes them upstream, where they find and release Mabon. Hidden between the lines of this story are two fundamental truths: if you move *upstream* you reach the source, the origin, and if the ancient salmon of wisdom feeds on the nuts of the sacred Hazel, the tree must be even older than the fish. The teaching is thus that if we find and connect with our laughing inner child, we will also be in tune with the oldest wisdom in the world.

In various traditions Hazel is generally believed to be governed by Mercury and Venus. In Greek and Roman myth the tree is associated with Hermes (the Roman Mercurius) whose staff is a hazel rod, known as the *caduceus* — two intertwined snakes on a hazel rod — which is still the symbol of the healing arts.

Hazel objects have also been found at Iron Age burial sites in northwest Europe, for example, bowls with nuts, necklaces and wands.

Inspiration

The number nine recurs frequently in connection with Hazel: the physical tree takes nine years to mature; the Connla's Well is surrounded by nine Hazel trees; Hazel gives inspiration and nine is the number of the Muses. Nine is also the sacred number of Gaia, the Spirit of the Earth.

Intellectually, the symbolism of the nut is easily understood. To 'crack a nut' means to solve a mystery, to find a hidden solution. The aura of Hazel when we visit it is simply cooling, refreshing, light, and youthful. It is undemanding. Hazel smiles with us, but on a deeper level Hazel holds the path to our own inner child. The psychological concept of the inner child, that part within us that has not forgotten how to play, laugh, wonder or recognize the magic of life, is paralleled by Mabon — the mythical child, who is forever young. The wisdom of Hazel tells us where this child is hidden.

Apple

Rose family: *Rosaceae*
Crab Apple *(Malus sylvestris)*
Cultivated Apple *(Malus domestica)*

Physical appearance

The Wild Apple or Crabtree is a tree of river glades and Hornbeam-Oak woodlands. Under human influence it also appears in wooded pastures and wild hedges. In England, it is scattered through most types of woodland with roughly one crab apple every ten acres.

Archeological finds of apples in human settlements are common from the Neolithic period onwards but many may come from cultivated plants. The Apple is the oldest cultivated tree in Europe.

All Apple trees are small, bushy trees with many branches. The bisexual flowers appear with the leaves in April and May and are white or pink in colour. As in all plants of the rose family (Pear, Cherry, Hawthorn, Blackthorn, Plum, Rose *et al)* the flowers are five-fold. The fruits of the Crab Apple are small, hard and sour. Cultivated apples are usually bigger and sweeter, and today, more than one thousand types are known worldwide.

As with all roses, the side buds bear flowers and fruit, giving these trees their density. Some of the twigs die off and are modified into thorns. The Crab Apple bears some too; only the cultivated forms do not. However, when they escape from the orchard their descendants soon develop many features of the wild form again.

Healing

Apples strengthen the whole metabolism, balance the digestion, stimulate blood production as well as the metabolism of fats, and cleanse the system. They also have diuretic, febrifugal and relaxing properties, and stimulate the appetite.

However, both cooked and raw apples should not be eaten in the evening, for they may start to ferment in the stomach overnight.

To treat diarrhoea, two to four finely grated apples, three times a day, help enormously, especially when supported by herbal teas. If the intestines need stimulation, fried or baked apples are the right things. Fresh and fried apples also stimulate the liver and kidneys. Fried apples are also good for a sore throat.

Apple skin tea stimulates the bladder and kidneys, relaxes the nervous system and reduces fever.

Remember the old adage: 'An apple a day keeps the doctor away!'

Bach Flower Therapy uses the wild form, the Crab Apple, which relates to perfection. People who have definite ideas about how they and the world around them should be — pure and flawless, — and who become pedantic, self-condemning and feel unclean as a result, can find relief through Crab Apple.

Tradition

Of all members of the rose family, the Apple has the richest and most mean-ingful mythology, apart from Hawthorn and the Rose itself.

We will omit the apple that Eve shared with Adam because the Hebrew original of *Genesis* only speaks of *peri* — a fruit — and not specifically an apple.

In Greek myth, Gaia, the goddess of the Earth, gives a sacred apple tree to the Queen of Heaven, Hera, when she marries Zeus. It is guarded in

Apple trees with mistletoe in November mist.

Apple trees.

the garden of the Hesperides by the sisters of that name, and by the watchful dragon, Ladon. It is one of Heracles' tasks to fetch some of this tree's fruit.

When Paris, Prince of Troy, was asked to make a choice between the three goddesses — Hera, Athena, and Aphrodite — he passed an apple to the latter, the supreme goddess of love and beauty, and the mother of Eros. The aspects of fertility and eroticism are thus contained in this all-encompassing symbol of life — the apple. Apples can be found in various love rituals, and fertility and marriage customs all over Western Europe. Apples also occur frequently in southern Slavic marriage customs.

In Asgard, the city of the gods in Norse myth, near the core of the World Tree, the magical apples, which bestow everlasting youth upon the Asir, are kept by Idun (a female Asir). This is reminiscent of the fruit or sap of the Tree of Life itself.

An important area in the Celtic Otherworld is *Tir Nan Og,* the Land of Eternal Youth. It is frequently described as an island in the western sea. In Arthurian legend, the dying king is last seen on a bark sailing towards the setting sun, to the Land of the Blessed called *Avalon.* Avalon means 'Apple.' It is striking that both the Greek and the Celtic Apple Island lie to the west, far beyond the sunset.

In this world, Avalon is the old name for the sacred hill at Glastonbury. The county of Somerset used to be marsh and wetland in the past. Nowadays, it is still famous for its apples (and cider!) but previously apple trees could only be grown on rare tracts of higher land. The Glastonbury Tor was supposedly surrounded by apple orchards.

Inspiration

The apple is the gift of life and eternal youth, which transports mortals to the land of the immortal — not only King Arthur, but also ordinary people. In a Welsh tale, a young farmer from Llanberis falls in love with a nymph from the nearby lake. He eventually lures her to him with an apple of rare and delicious quality, and they marry. An apple in myth is the ticket to cross from one world to another. In this sense even the early translators of the Bible, by substituting the unspecified 'fruit' (Hebrew) in the original story with the Apple, were in accordance with pre-Christian lore. Here, too, the (in this case unjustified) possession of the fruit facilitates a change of reality.

Ivy

Aralia family: *Araliaceae*
Ivy *(Hedera helix)*

Physical appearance

Ivy is not a tree; it is one of the few climbers in the temperate woodlands of the northern hemisphere where it carpets the ground or climbs on trees, rocks or walls, up to a height of 20 m (65 feet). Contrary to common belief, it does not strangle the trees it grows on, although fully grown it can deprive them of light. Ivy itself can live with minimal light, for example, carpeting the ground in Beech woods, as well as thriving on various soil types. It grows slowly and can live for hundreds of years.

Ivy. Pen and ink drawing.

Ivy has two kinds of shoots. The climbing shoots send out tiny rootlets that take hold on the surface the plant climbs on. These shoots have three or five-lobed leaves, which are shiny and dark green with a network of white veins. The second kind of shoots, only occur in certain amounts of light and cannot climb. These have heart-shaped or elliptical, pointed leaves and carry the flowers. The clusters of yellow-green flowers appear in the autumn and the three to five seeds within each black berry mature by early spring.

The other members of its botanical family are found in the tropics.

Healing

The fruits are nutritious for birds (blackbird, thrush), which distribute the seeds, but they are poisonous to humans as well as horses. The leaves, however, were collected as fodder for livestock from Neolithic times until the sixteenth century, hence its German name *Efeu*, from the Middle High German, from *ep-heu*, *heu* (hay).

Generally the leaves of the reproductive ivy branches are effective on the lower part of the human body, such as the spleen or on corns. The star-shaped leaves of the high climbing branches are effective on the head area, for ear and eye problems, loosening mucus in sinusitis and bronchitis. Decoctions of leaves for internal use should only be taken after consulting your local supplier of homeopathic [ivy] products.

Tradition

In ancient Egypt, Ivy was dedicated to the lord of vegetation, Osiris. Similarly, along with the Vine, it was sacred to the wildest and most ecstatic of the Greek vegetation gods, Dionysos, The priests and followers of Dionysos would wear ivy wreaths for ceremonies and subsequent drinking sessions. Dionysos was called Bacchus by the Romans and his cult spread across Europe. Cups made of ivy wood were believed to reveal wine of bad quality and to counterbalance the unwanted side effects of alcohol. In the Middle Ages, ivy leaves mashed in vinegar with a hint of rose water, were used to soothe a hangover. Well into the nineteenth century, many English pubs still had a big ivy wreath hanging outside.

Fertility symbol surrounded by Ivy.

Inspiration

Alcohol brings the life energy down to the lower part of the body, but the climbing Ivy works in exactly the opposite way, particularly if the ivy is worn as a wreath around the head. A *crown* on the head concentrates our minds, will power and consciousness, especially if the crown is made of fresh leaves still vibrant with life.

Although the cult of Dionysos was notorious for its debauchery, its origins were probably very different. Under priestly supervision, the drinking of wine was a communion with the Spirit of the Vine (Dionysos), who, in warm regions, was a close ally of the deity of vegetation. Ivy was invited along to filter out certain effects of the alcohol. Shamans in South America or southern Asia still use alcohol to reach trance states. Ivy seems to be part of a secret knowledge of alchemy which has been lost in the West.

In parts of England and Wales, Ivy is widely seen as the female counterpart of the male Holly. Branches of both are brought into the house at Christmas; the 'Holly Boy' complimenting the 'Ivy Girl' in the traditional Christmas carol.

Ivy's function in nature, however, is rather obscure to modern humankind. Widely believed to be a parasite (which it is not), it does not gain much sympathy, particularly from tree lovers. However, Ivy actually protects the wood from the harmful effects of some forms of radiation. In many places the increase of Ivy over past decades parallels the increase in microwave pollution. Even if Ivy competes with its carrier tree for light, and might eventually kill branches or the whole tree, without Ivy the tree might die even earlier!

Ivy gave up its potential for size and stateliness or famous fruits. It discarded these possibilities for flexibility and adaptability, and covers what is dead and ugly, like ruins or waste ground, or what needs protecting. It is like the good and modest child in the fairy tales, doing what needs to be done. The Ivy is a true daughter of Gaia, the Earth Spirit.

Blackthorn

Rose family: *Rosaceae*
Blackthorn *(Prunus spinosa)*

Physical appearance

Blackthorn is an extremely dense, almost impenetrable bush, rarely higher than four metres (12 feet), which spreads horizontally. Its far-reaching roots produce numerous suckers and so Blackthorn can create wide thickets 'through which nobody larger than a rabbit can pass' (Rackham 1980). This is mainly due to its long and very sharp spines, which offers perfect shelter for small nesting birds.

Blackthorn flowers early in April, well before its small, oval leaves unfold. The myriads of small, white, bisexual flowers have five petals (rose family). The round fruits (sloes) ripen late in the autumn and are a deep bluish-black colour, hence their old Germanic name, *sleha* (bluish).

Blackthorn grows in light or half-shade, and is quite modest in terms of soil. In the temperate zone it is the most widespread of the *prunus* trees. Other members of this family are cultivars like Cherry and, in southern Europe, Peach, Apricot and Almond.

Blackthorn blossoms.

Blackthorn.

Healing

The remains of sloe stones have been found in ash from Mesolithic (*c.* 8000–2700 BC) and Iron Age sites, implying that they formed part of early man's diet. Today, in the West, we are spoilt by easy access to our food. It is simply too much bother to try separating the bit of flesh from the large stone inside the sloe, and they are incredibly bitter.

However, those who make the effort will certainly be rewarded. Sloes clean the blood and stimulate the whole metabolism, and are astringent and laxative. The flowers are also laxative, diuretic and clean the blood. Blackthorn helps with indigestion; skin problems, such as eczema, herpes and allergies; colds and catarrh. In the past, Blackthorn preparations were also used for neurosis, weak heart, kidney stones, and bladder and prostate problems.

Traditionally, sloes were gathered after the first frosts, which leached some of the bitterness from the fruits, but in today's changing climate waiting for the first frost in many areas can take us right into the New Year. You can ignore this and just pick them when they feel ripe. Sloes can be prepared as juice, syrup, jelly, jam, wine and the spirit, sloe gin. Follow ordinary recipes, remembering to add some extra sweetening. Sloes are best combined with apples when making jam, or can be added in small quantities to a mixed fruit jam. The main problem in cooking with sloes is the stones, which have to be strained off.

To make sloe gin wash 450 g (1 lb) of stalk-less sloes, prick them with a needle and place in a screw-top bottle. Add 75–100 g (3–4 oz) of sugar and a few drops of almond flavouring, and fill the bottle with gin. Screw the lid on tightly and leave in a dark place for three months, shaking occasionally. After this time, strain the liquid until clear and re-bottle.

Tradition

Blackthorn hardly appears in myth, but is more common in folklore. Its flowers and thorns display beauty and armour, life and death, light and shadow. The shamanic world-view of the tribal peoples had no problems with understanding the unity of these forces, but later, the division of nature into good and evil introduced condemnation.

Blackthorn was certainly on the dark side, and during the Christian era its negative image as a dark, hostile, *witch* tree was established. Its harsh-tasting fruit, sharp thorns, and inhospitable shape also made it a convenient target for suspicions of all kinds. The devil must have spoilt this ugly tree! Witches were, for example, believed to drive blackthorn spikes into wax figures, to bring pain or death to other people. The devil himself was believed to initiate his followers by pricking them with a thorn.

However, in Eastern Europe, which was more remote from the Church of Rome, Blackthorn maintained a much more positive image, and Blackthorn or its thorns were believed to protect against witches and other evil. In a Baltic tale from what is now Poland, one night God showered the Blackthorn with white flowers as a sign of its innocence.

Inspiration

In nature Blackthorn is a natural guardian tree, and can isolate places by creating impenetrable barriers through which no one can pass. Consequently, Blackthorn teaches us to respect boundaries. By crossing lines that we should not cross we bring pain to others. The burning of witches and heretics on blackthorn pyres is a classic example of this.

Blackthorn cleanses both body and soul. On the physical plane, a stimulated metabolism disperses toxins in the body. On the psychological plane, too, old wounds and impurities come to the surface to be transformed. Thus Blackthorn confronts us with our own *dark* side.

Elder

Honeysuckle family: *Caprifoliaceae*
Elder *(Sambucus nigra)*

Physical appearance

Elders usually grow in the shape of bushes, rarely trees. The paired leaves are oval to elliptical in shape, and the five to seven leaflets have sharply toothed edges. The twigs contain soft, white pith. The strongly scented, creamy white, bisexual flowers appear in June in large, circular groups. In early autumn these clusters hang heavily from the tree, loaded with shiny black juicy berries (red in the Red-berried Elder).

Elder can be found in open woods, on riverbanks, in gardens and in hedgerows. On waste ground or near a compost heap where soil is nitrogen rich, Elder — often with stinging nettle — helps to rebalance the soil. Elder's roots first spread horizontally, checking for nutrients, and then go deeper. The leaves often have a slightly unpleasant smell — similar to the organic substances that the tree transforms — but its sweetly scented flowers reveal that the Elder can change the raw into the noble. The gentle Elder has a tough aspect, as it originates primarily from a gnarled root, which can bring forth shoots time and time again.

Healing

Elder and Lime are the only two trees of which every part is benevolent to man: bark, root, leaves, flowers and fruits. They are the great healing trees of the temperate climate.

The berries of Elder are rich in vitamins and strengthen the immune system. They ripen before the waves of colds and flu come in the autumn, and can be preserved as juice, wine, syrup or jam. Hot elderberry juice is a splendid prophylaxis against flu and is also antiseptic. The berries are cooked for a few minutes and then pressed and strained. The hot beverage is sweetened with honey.

The flowers, too, are helpful for colds since they are sudorific, febrifugal and relaxing. For tea, use one or two teaspoons of flowers per cup of water. At the summer solstice, Elderflower pancakes, a traditional meal in parts of Central Europe, are simply delicious. Prepare normal pancake batter. Before it has cooked completely place a flower head in the frying pan and leave it in the pancake. Fry slowly while the elder aroma permeates the pancake. The flowers are eaten as well, though the stalks should be discarded.

Elderflower juice makes a healthy, refreshing summer drink. Seven big flower heads — or more, according to taste — and two to three sliced lemons are left overnight in seven litres (15 pints) of cold water. The following day, boil the mixture with 20 g (1 oz) of tartaric acid (which can be left out to get a fizzy drink), then strain, sweeten according to taste with about 1 kg (2 lb) of sugar or honey, and poured into bottles. Drink cold in the summer. If you want to keep it longer, bring to the boil again after straining, and make sure the bottles are airtight. Elderberry and elderflower wine are probably the most well known uses for Elder in Great Britain. There are many different recipes for both types of wine.

Elderberries.

Elders by Martin Klatt.

Bark, root and leaves were all used as remedies in the past. The leaves give off a smell which is unpleasant to insects, and can be used — to a certain extent — to keep insects away, by rubbing elder leaves on your skin.

The homeopathic *Sambucus* is an important remedy in the treatment of infection. It is used for irrational fears, arising particularly at night during sleep, which may be psychosomatic symptoms of another infection.

Tradition

The Elder is the tree of the Great Goddess, who in northern Europe was known as *Holla*. The tree's Old High German name *holun tar* means 'tree of

Elder.

Holla.' She appears in the fairy tale of *Frau Holle* (collected by the Brothers Grimm), where she is the archetypal, well-meaning wise mother. Holla embodies the nourishing and healing aspects of the Earth Mother.

Far and wide Elder was regarded as the dwelling place of the good house spirit, the invisible guardian of house and farmyard. In the eighteenth and nineteenth centuries, many customs still believed in the protective powers of Elder, and the benevolence of this tree was appreciated by the people amongst whom it grew: the Swedes offered milk; the Prussians, bread and beer, and the Scots left cakes and milk in its shade.

Other Celts, as well as Slavs, also paid their respects to the Danish *Hyllemoer* (Elder Mother). She protected house dwellers from bad luck and illness, and her tree was never to be cut down, nor its wood burnt. 'Hats off to the Elder!' was a widespread farmer's saying in Switzerland and parts of Germany (Stäubli 1927, 262). If its wood did have to be cut, it was preceded by a prayer, for example: 'Lady Elder, give me some of thy wood; then will I give thee, also, some of mine when it grows in the forest' (Mannhardt 1877).

The Swedes said that on midsummer night under an elder bush you could see the elfin king and his court pass by. Generally, customs and tales reflect the notion that the Elder is the threshold to the subterranean world of earth spirits. The old Frisians buried their dead under elder trees, and many customs employed this tree for burial rites. In the early twentieth century, Austrian Tyroleans still carried a cross of elder wood before the coffin, and then placed it on the grave (Stäubli 1927, 266).

As a guardian of the threshold the Swedish *Hyllefroa* (Elder Woman) was also associated with birth and fertility. An old view of the incredible power and grace of Elder is best preserved in a Russian tradition. Major diseases and the causes of death are personified by Twelve Maidens (in some traditions nine) who come over the ocean, climb the sacred mountain and there gain the agreement of the *Three Elders* that all living things are subject to death. This story would be sung by the women of a village which was threatened by an epidemic, while they used a plough to draw a furrow around the village, as a barrier against the evil spirits:

> Within these boiling cauldrons
> Every life under the sky
> Burns with indelible fire [lit by the Twelve Maidens]
> Around the boiling cauldrons
> The old Elder trees stand.
> The old Elders sing —
> They sing of life, they sing of death,
> They sing of the whole human race.
> The old Elders bestow
> Long life on the whole world;
> But to the other, the bad death,
> The old Elders command
> A long and far journey.
> The old Elders promise
> Eternal life
> To the whole of Humankind.
>   (Mannhardt 1877, 15f).

Inspiration

This Russian song invokes the mercy of the threefold Great Goddess, demanding a long and healthy life. The Elder is the hand, ear and mouth of the creator for the protection of the living. The Elder Mother carries us to the gate of death, where she soothes our fear of the unknown, and brings us gently towards the tunnel of light.

Lime leaves.

Lime bark.

Lime (Linden)

Lime family: *Tiliaceae*
Small-leaved Lime *(Tilia cordata)*
Large-leaved Lime *(Tilia platyphyllos)*

Physical appearance

Limes or Lindens are among the most beautiful and tallest deciduous trees of the temperate zone. The Small-leaved Lime is native to all of Europe and western Russia. The Large-leaved Lime has a distribution that is slightly more southerly. They cross-fertilize where they meet, resulting in the Common Lime *(Tilia vulgaris),* which is often found in parks and avenues. These trees are closely related to the American Linden and Basswood trees.

The root system of this tree is very deep. Lime connects firmly with the ground through many roots. It loves warmth and moisture, which it needs to maintain its dense foliage. Lime trees reach many hundreds of, and occasionally more than one thousand, years of age.

The paired, rather large leaves are heart-shaped with sharply toothed edges. The foliage in midsummer is sometimes populated by tiny aphids, which exude sticky *honeydew*. The leaves turn yellow and golden in the early autumn.

The strongly scented, light yellow to greenish flowers have five sepals and five petals, and are bisexual. The stalk of the flower clusters carries a wing-like, papery bract, which later helps to distribute the seed. At flowering time in June and July, Limes are visited by countless bumble-bees and honey-bees, which work the flowers vigorously and noisily, hence its American name, *Bee Tree*. The fruit is a round, hard, downy nut.

The wide crowns of solitary trees protect the trunk from direct sunlight, but Lime can also form woodland. In the mixed oak woods of ancient times, Lime was a dominant tree. Later, many of these woodlands changed to beech woods.

> The scented limewoods in July, heavy with blossom and humming with bees, with their pale bluish leaves and yellow bracts, are an astonishing and glorious sight; but they hide down obscure lanes and nobody celebrates them (Rackham 1980, 237).

Lime woods are often enhanced by a ground cover of bluebells, primroses or wood anemones.

Healing

The benevolence of Lime can only possibly be surpassed by Elder. Lime (Linden) *soothes*; the German verb *lindern* (to soothe) is derived from it. In Classical times, it was an important healing tree: the Greek centaur, Chiron, gained such fame as a physician and prophet that he was given the title *Son of Philyria* — Philyria was the mother spirit of Lime.

Flowers, leaves and bark have sudorific, febrifugal, cramp loosening and antiseptic effects, and are mainly used for fever and colds. One teaspoon of flowers per cup of water can be drunk according to demand. Three to six cups daily are recommended. The flower tea is also used for catarrh and slight skin infections, or in compresses for inflamed or tired eyes.

The wood ash of Lime makes a disinfectant tooth powder that also strengthens the gums. In the past it was also used to cure liver and gall-bladder problems, heartburn, diseases of the digestive tract and menstrual problems.

Young lime leaves, as well as the buds and flowers, can be eaten in salads or soups. Dried flowers are best kept in small linen or cotton sacks.

Tradition

Lime wood is moderately hard and excellent for carving. Some Native Americans carve totem masks in this wood, which are then used for healing ceremonies (Storl 1997).

Lime has another practical use: its phloem fibres are especially tough and flexible, and were used by ancient Greeks or Anglo-Saxons alike; ropes, mats, bags and clothes can be made from it. The Anglo-Saxons called the tree *linde*, but had a second name, *bæst*, to denote the coppice stools, which were cut on a rotation of fourteen to fifteen years for the harvest of bast (Rackham 1980). The economic pressure for these fibres was such that hemp (cannabis) was also planted for this purpose thus relieving the young *bæst* trees.

In many Germanic tribes an old Lime tree was used as the *omphalos*, the central pole and meeting point for communal affairs. They believed that criminals receiving sentences were softened by the soothing atmosphere of this tree. Lime was seen as generating divine knowledge, truth, justice, clarity, a balance of decisiveness and compassion. It was dedicated to *Freya*, the Mistress of the Earth and goddess of love.

In Scandinavia, Lime was the most important of the three *Varträd*, the guardian trees of house and farmyard, which received regular offerings of gratitude, and gave their names to many families — Lindemann, Tiliander, Linné.

The tradition of the Lime as a tribal tree developed into the German *Dorflinde*, the village lime tree, which was cared for, often visited and well loved; the tradition was still alive in the nineteenth century as it was in medieval times.

The ancient Teutons, however, met under trees to receive impulses from the world of spirit. The soothsayers of the ancient Scythians practised divination using Lime bark, and Graves gives similar evidence from ancient Greece (Philpot 1994, 102; Graves 1975, 2.236). However, in the Age of Reason, poetry and tree paintings, emotions and dreams were treated with contempt.

A peculiar incident occurs in the *Legend of Sigurd,* a Norse hero of equal importance to the Irish Cuchulan. He slays a dragon and bathes in its blood since it has the power to bestow invulnerability, but one of the trees above him drops a leaf that lands between his shoulder blades, and creates a soft spot that he does not know about. However, the traitor who eventually slays him does. Since the Middle Ages the tree in question is believed to have been Lime.

Inspiration

Since the development of heraldry in the twelfth century some European nations, particularly England and Germany, have identified with their 'male' Oak. However, while authorities align themselves with the powers of lion, eagle and Oak, the heart of the common people often balance this. In Germany, the counterbalance for pride in the Oak was the people's affection for the 'female' Lime tree.

In the *Legend of Sigurd*, the Lime also has a balancing role. In the heroic age the warrior did not live for success, but for his honour that was valued

more highly than wealth or life. It was the spiritual code of the tribal warrior to live up to his inner truth in a dignified and sincere way, and he did not relinquish these values to fear of death or failure. A magic potion of invulnerability is, therefore, *cheating*, and Sigurd would have been unhappy for the rest of his life. By shedding its leaf, the tree acts on behalf of Sigurd's higher self, as an act of mercy.

This legend further reveals that the gentle Lime grows close to the wild dragon's den. Old words for dragon — the German *Lindwurm*; Old English *lindworm* — and the name of the tree have a common root, the Indo-European *lentos* (flexible). In all cultures the dragon is a personification of the Earth's life force, which flows along the *dragon* or *ley* lines. A person encountering a place of intense Earth or *dragon* energy is charged both physically and spiritually. All over the world, such places have been known for millennia as sacred places and were used for quests or ritual; it thus seems that Sigurd went to a sacred Lime wood on his quest.

Despite its soft appearance, Lime has the power to put us in touch with the life force of the Earth, but it will always channel the power of the dragon in a calm, soothing, healing and merciful way. Lime is the place where Heaven and Earth meet. When you cannot concentrate, when your energies are in disarray, you can find calm and stillness in the presence of Lime.

Lime woods.

Spruce

Pine family: *Pinaceae*
Norway Spruce *(Picea abies)*

Physical appearance

In the history of the Earth, conifers have been around much longer than deciduous trees. They are tougher and more adaptable to harsh conditions. They loose less water than leafy trees and can survive in regions with short, warm seasons since they do not recreate their entire foliage each year. Their needles start to photosynthesize in early spring, much earlier than deciduous trees. The branches allow snow to glide off, and many trees possess some form of biological *anti-freeze*. Worldwide, there are many species of Spruce and Fir, each finely adjusted to the climate of their particular region. Let us take a closer look at the Norway Spruce and Silver Fir as representatives of the large group of conifers.

Norway Spruce has, like the Silver Fir, an upright and conical shape. Each year the trunk gains a new whorl of branches. Its needles stand on little pegs projecting from the twig, and when they fall they leave these pegs behind, which makes bare Spruce twigs very rough to the touch. The needles stay on the tree for five years or more, and every June sets of new needles fringe all the branches.

Pure Spruce stands, whether natural or planted, have a dark, overwhelming impression, but a natural Spruce wood has more space to breathe. Old trees have a more open, rugged crown, and form a multi-layered forest with young trees, in which some leafy trees may appear as well. Spruce can dominate vast areas, particularly in northern conifer woodlands.

Spruce thrives in the mountains at heights of 1,300–2,400 metres (4,300–7,900 feet). Spruce can bear the cold, acidic soil and a certain amount of dryness, but not the heat. It also shies away from mild, Atlantic winters. Norway Spruce has naturally colonized a vast wooded belt from the Norwegian Atlantic coast to the Siberian Pacific coast, and has been introduced to most parts of North America.

As a robust tree, Spruce was the saviour during necessary reforestation in eighteenth and nineteenth century Europe, and again after the two world wars in the twentieth century. Spruce grows quickly, making it the top tree in Europe's forest economies. The Sitka Spruce, grows even faster, but the Norway Spruce can adapt to drought and the cold better. With heights of fifty metres (180 feet) and more some of the spruce in the foothills of the Alps are among the tallest native trees in Europe, but not of their family — Sitka can reach 60 m (200 feet); Grand Fir up to 100 m (350 feet). Spruce also creates a lot of raw humus on the ground, and can be destroyed by fire or insect pandemics.

The root system of Spruce is rather shallow on poor soils, but in rich, deep soils it reaches far down. The tree can hold on to rocks or create a root cushion on marshland, which is sufficient for survival, but on flat ground the tree is threatened by wind. Most species of Spruce, as well as Fir, live for hundreds of years.

The flowers of both sexes are found on the same tree. Norway Spruce only flowers every three to four years, and in mountain areas only about every seven years. The small, round, male catkins are red at first but become yellow in May. The female flowers — small, oval and erect — are usually found higher up the tree. The fertilized cones gradually turn until in the

Fir wood.

Spruce by Per-Olaf Mademann.

autumn they are long, pendant, cylindrical cones. After many of the winged seeds are released, the cones drop to the ground.

The cone of Silver Fir stays erect throughout its life. In most Fir species the single scales fall off after releasing the small, winged seeds, and only the bare spindle remains on the twig. Fir needles are flatter and longer than those of Spruce, and dark green with two silvery bands on the underside. On later twigs the needles spread horizontally, giving the branches the appearance of broad layers. When the needles drop after six or more years the little pegs drop too, leaving the twig smooth, unlike Spruce.

Both Fir and Spruce naturally start their life in the shadow of the mother trees. Its ability to cope with shade allows Fir to grow beneath Beech or Spruce. Fir trees are native to the moist mixed woodlands of the southern and central European mountains, where they can be found at altitudes of up to 1,830 metres (6,000 feet). Fir stabilizes slopes and protects them from erosion, but is very sensitive to air pollution, as well as to grazing animals.

Healing

The buds of most conifer species contain high amounts of resin and essential oil. Fir has been used for healing since Classical times. Resin, needles, buds and shoots were mainly applied in the treatment of gout, rheumatism, bronchitis and infections of the mouth and throat. The buds are still used today to soothe coughs and loosen mucus. They are antiseptic and stimulate circulation (about one teaspoon of buds boiled for a short time in one cupful of water; three to four cups daily). However, they can irritate the skin in some cases. For a Spruce bath boil 150–200 g (6–7 oz) of needles in one litre (2 pints) of water, strain and add to the bath water.

The smoke of wood or resin has a cleansing effect on rooms, as does the vaporized essential oil.

Tradition

Four important substances are extracted from Spruce and Pine: pitch, tar, resin and turpentine. These substances served to waterproof all kinds of wood and to seal ships and timbers, as well as supplying fuel for oil lamps. The Latin name, *picea* (pitch), still reflects this time-honoured use. The English term, *Spruce*, derives from *Pruce* which denoted the origin of the first timber of this kind imported to England from Prussia, in the sixteenth century. In old sources, as well as legends, Spruce and Fir are used synonymously, and mostly refer to Fir trees.

Spruce wood is generally not as good as that of Fir, but particularly slow-growing mountain trees traditionally provided wood for the soundboards of musical instruments.

The ancient Greeks dedicated the Fir to Poseidon, god of the sea, probably because ships' masts were made from its trunks.

Most sacred trees and groves in history were deciduous, but conifers also received their share of veneration. In fourth century Gaul, Bishop Martin of Tours, who was the first Christian to violate sacred groves, demolished a temple unopposed, but when he tried to cut down the nearby sacred Fir tree he was prevented from doing so.

In Poland, a female spirit called a Dziwitza, a huntress like the Roman Diana, was said to roam the Fir woods. Another female wood spirit, Boruta, was said to inhabit Fir trees. The Spirit or King of the Forest, whose voice is heard in the murmur of the breeze and the rustle of the leaves, is always depicted carrying an uprooted fir tree, both in local legends and tales of

Eastern Europe and the Alpine region. He also dwells in one of the oldest Firs within his territory.

Evergreens have always held a special position in the eyes of humankind as embodiments of everlasting power, which promises the return of light and spring. An ancient custom at midwinter, the longest night of the year, is to decorate an evergreen tree with lights and spheres representing celestial influences, nuts and apples to represent the fertility of the coming new year, and sweets for the sweetness of extrasensory, holy vision. The Silver Fir played a central role in the return of this tradition in the guise of the Christmas tree. Despite the disapproval of the Church it quickly acquired enormous fame. Most conifers sold today as Christmas trees are, however, Spruce.

Inspiration

Conifers are completely dominated by Saturn, and the forces that inhibit growth processes, contract substance and harden form. The way in which the branches of a conifer focus tightly around the central trunk, just as the needles do around the twig, are further expressions of these forces. Conifers do not extend far into the surrounding space like deciduous trees do. The very needle shape only allows the smallest possible contact with the environment. Saturn governs the conifers, and many of them reach sexual maturity only after the planet has performed one full cycle (about thirty years). Saturn's long rhythm also grants them long life. With their confined, hard shapes they can venture deeper into the winter, into the mountains and into the north than any other tree or shrub.

Spruce and Fir belong to the mountains. Not many trees would dare to venture into these high regions, which are, in some ways, closer to certain celestial forces than to the Earth. The old cultures saw the divine plan unfolding from the mountain tops downwards, the Greek deities of Mount Olympus, and the Germanic Asir, are described as dwelling on high ridges. The Incas built Macchu Pichu in an extraordinarily high location, not to mention the sacred mountains of the Native Americans or the Himalayas. Conifers have such an intimate part in the exchange of these mighty forces that their shape displays an even geometry that is reminiscent of the molecular structure of crystals or the physical patterns of starlight. These 'green snowflakes' are much closer to the mineral world than their deciduous relatives.

Sometimes, a single fir or spruce reached an extraordinary age and size, and people immediately felt that such a tree had developed a more individual spirit. Such a tree often became known by a special name, which might be as simple as *The Old Fir,* and was highly respected. In the nineteenth century, there was such a tree at Tarssok, Russia. When it finally died the country people declined to profit from the sale of its huge trunk, and donated the money to the church (Folkard 1892, 337).

Walking through natural conifer woods gives a feeling of deep calm and peace. Spruce and Fir also have a strong physiological effect on us: their pungent oils tone and heal our lungs, just by roaming through the scented woods.

Nowadays, mountain conifers are abused in huge monocultures in regions completely unsuitable for them — low altitudes with wet, mild winters. Worse still, they are not even allowed to reach maturity, let alone old age.

Larch

Pine family: *Pinaceae*
Common or European Larch *(Larix deciduas)*

Physical appearance

Larch is a fast-growing, tall tree of mountainous areas up to 2,000 m (6,500 feet), and sub-arctic regions, and thrives in cool, moist and harsh climates. It can survive in barren soil but needs a lot of light and, with its loose crown and light foliage, is a typical light tree. Larch contains a lot of vitality and regenerative power within its slender, upright trunk. It is adapted for heavy

Larch.

storms with its branches having deliberate breaking points at their bases. Single branches break off at the predetermined points before the whole tree is endangered. The trunk then produces new shoots to close the gap.

Unlike its nearest relatives, Fir, Spruce and Pine, the Larch sheds its needle-like leaves in the autumn, having turned to a golden straw colour. In the spring new, emerald green needles unfold, which later become darker but remain soft. They stand in tufts of about twenty or thirty.

Both sexes of flowers are found on the same tree, a little before the needles. The males are yellow, drooping cones. The females are soft, rosy-pink upright cones, which later harden, and turn into cylindrical cones with brown closed scales. After shedding the seeds in the autumn of the same year as fertilization occurred, the empty cones stay on the tree for several more years.

The wood of Larch is harder and more durable and resinous than that of Spruce, Fir and Pine.

Healing

As long ago as the first century AD, Pliny the Elder knew how to prepare larch ointment. This remedy, made from the resin, helps rheumatism, gout, skin infections and particularly problems with the respiratory system. A larch needle bath is as benevolent as one of Spruce, Fir or Pine. Internally, larch resin stimulates the kidneys, although too much can irritate them. A small ball of resin can be chewed safely to soothe coughs, throat problems, etc. (see also Spruce and Pine).

In Bach Flower Therapy, Larch awakens and enhances self-confidence. People, who are convinced of their inferiority, deprive themselves of the best things in life, remaining with feelings of discouragement and melancholy. Larch helps overcome these limitations, encouraging the person to take the first steps and persevere, climbing seemingly high mountains.

Tradition

Western European legends concerning Larch are confined to Alpine regions, which are the areas of its natural distribution. Larch is frequently described as the abode of the *Säligen* (the blessed ones), a race of graceful, elf-like beings who live inside the mountains, are kind to people and protect animals. Their culture and invisible settlements mirror the Irish elfin race, often referred to as the *Tuatha Dé Danann,* or the *fir sidhe.*

In different parts of the Alps, spirits called the *Salgfräulein* (blessed maidens), were said to have been seen many times sitting under an old larch, dressed all in white or silver like the snow on the mountain tops, and singing the sweetest music, which could sometimes even be heard in the valleys. (Porteous 1996, 93; Mannhardt 1875, 99f)

Consequently, larch wood was used for talismans and as cleansing incense. Until 1859, a sacred Larch stood at Nauders in the Austrian Tyrol. No one would dare to quarrel or swear near it, and if inclined to do so be warned by his fellows: 'Don't, the sacred tree is here!' (Porteous 1996, 217).

In Siberia, among the Ostiaks, a group of seven larch trees was regarded as a sacred grove (Porteous 1996, 54).

Inspiration

Everything that is hardened, stiff and dark in Spruce is soft, delicate and light in Larch. Its overall appearance is more rounded than the typical conifer, its needles are soft, and its cones are pink. It brightens up Spruce woods and mixed woodlands (with Pine, Birch, Aspen, Alder and Oak) with its spring emerald and autumn gold. Larch makes a tremendous step towards leafy trees, by renewing its foliage annually, and possessing the ability to modify its crown from symmetrical geometry to more expressive shapes otherwise only achieved by deciduous trees.

Larch has the potential for individuality, which is reflected in local legend and folklore. The Larch is the home of graceful, benevolent beings — *the blessed ones* — who belong to another, timeless plane of existence. Under a larch we can experience their peace and merriment.

Overleaf: Larch by Per-Olaf Mademann.

Pine

Pine family: *Pinaceae*
Scots Pine *(Pinus sylvestris)*

Physical appearance

The Scots Pine is extraordinarily versatile, and easily recognized by the fiery red hues of its bark, which blend into grey-browns towards the base. Owing to its great flexibility it can master most extremes: dry, sandy or poor soils to moist, boggy soils; stormy coastlines and continental valleys; as well as extreme cold and even some heat. In the Alps, it can grow at altitudes up to 2,200 m (7,300 feet). On extremely poor soils, Pine can be a pioneer tree,

Pine. Woodcut by Maxine Relton.

alongside birch and willows. It lives in close symbiosis with fungi, which create the necessary minerals for the tree. There are about one hundred species of Pine in the northern hemisphere. They are tough trees used to a variety of conditions, but all of them need a lot of light.

The distinctive long, blue-green needles of the Scots Pine stand for two to three years in pairs around the twig. Young trees are conical while mature trees have a high crown of umbrella-like levels, with the lower half of the trunk largely free of branches. The overall shape is very much determined by local conditions. The root system is far-reaching but not dense.

Scots Pine can grow quickly, and has thus become the most common plantation tree in Europe. If it is not cut down for the production of furniture, telegraph poles, fences, construction work, boxes, wood wool or paper it can live for about three hundred years. Plantation owners who prefer their forests to be in straight lines are probably happier with the Norway Spruce, since the sociable Scots Pine attracts various types of undergrowth, such as Buckthorn, Rowan, Bramble. Even Spruce and deciduous trees appear since Scots Pine does not exhaust the light, moisture or nutrient supplies of its stand. In Siberia and Scandinavia, Scots Pine often socializes with Larch, Spruce, Birch and Aspen.

The Scots Pine is of great importance for red deer, pine martens, red squirrels, birds, as well as mice, voles, wood wasps and wood ants.

After about thirty years, the Scots Pine reaches sexual maturity and then carries male and female flowers on one tree. The male flowers are small, globular cones, which are yellow with pollen. The female cones appear at the ends of shoots and are pinkish purple. Fertilization takes place one year after pollination. Then the female flowers develop into woody pine cones of roughly three inches in length, which often still cling to the tree after the seeds have fallen out in the second year of maturation.

Healing

The healing properties of Pine's resin, bud shoots and needles have been known and venerated for a long time. They soothe coughs, help to expel bronchial phlegm, clear the head of congestion, enhance circulation, and are disinfectant, diuretic and relaxing. The resin vapours, which can also be inhaled from the living tree, stimulate the lungs and — like Larch, Fir and Spruce — are used to treat colds, coughs, flu, sore throats, bronchitis, pneumonia and asthma. This is done in the form of inhalations, ointments, teas and baths. Pine also has a strengthening effect on digestion and is a general revitalizing tonic. Pine products are available at the local chemist or health shop, but some can be produced at home.

A three or four litre saucepan is filled with dried or fresh bud shoots, topped up with water, and boiled for ten minutes. This can then be used straight away as an inhalation, or can be strained and added to bath water. A pine bath relaxes and strengthens the skin as well as the nervous system. For tea, pour one cup of boiling water over two teaspoons of pine shoots and leave to infuse for ten minutes. Do not drink more than one to two cups during the day.

The young buds are a tasty addition to salads, or can be preserved in honey.

The Bach Flower Remedy relates to guilt and self-blame, turning these feelings to forgiveness, self-acceptance and strength.

Tradition

Like Spruce and Fir, Pine has a long history of supplying people with pitch, tar, resin and turpentine. In Germany, the Scots Pine was also employed as an alternative to candles: a finger-sized shaving of pine wood, dipped into pitch or resin, burned for quite a while. This was not so common in England, where the Romans had exhausted most of the natural pine stands, which is why the modern name is *Scots* Pine. The needles can be burnt as incense room cleaning. Hippocrates was known to have used pine incense for healing.

Surprisingly, the myths of the northern forest tribes do not mention this tree. However, because of the long list of its practical gifts we can assume that Pine must have existed in the spiritual life of the people, even if no record remains. Its old names were discarded in the early Middle Ages and a new term, stemming from the Latin, *poena*, related to pain and punishment, was introduced into Germanic and Celtic with Christianity, and applied first in English to the pains of hell. Only a Finnish Christian tale, in which the Pine originates from the blood of the Saviour, indicates an old tradition of high respect.

In Greek and Roman myth, however, Pine appears frequently, though it is southern species that are mentioned — Maritime Pine *(Pinus pinaster)*, Stone Pine *(Pinus pinea)*, Aleppo Pine *(Pinus halepensis)*, Corsican Pine *(Pinus nigra* subsp. *laricio)* and so on. Pine was sacred to the ancient mother goddess, Cybele, who saved her consort, Attis, by turning him into a Pine tree. Pine was also dedicated to Zeus (Jupiter) as well as to Pan, the chief spirit of vegetation.

Later, in the Scottish Highlands, the Scots Pine appeared as the 'tree of the warriors,' marking their burial grounds (Fife 1994). No less than eight Scottish clans have Pine as their clan badge, making it the tree most often chosen for this purpose. As Viking and Norse warriors often received ship burials, we can also suppose that the Pine had some significance for them too, as it was fundamental to ship building.

Inspiration

In the mild climate of the south, the Pine is an embodiment of the Lord of Vegetation himself, in the cults of Attis and Pan, which have very different origins. As such it is an evergreen, imbued with spirit all year round, symbolizing the everlasting force of life.

In the rough northern climate, Pine reveals another aspect; here it becomes a victorious warrior, with a strong will to live. He stands up to the severity and impact of the elements, and thrives regardless of them, or the poorness of the soil or even rock, on which he stands. Pine has been one of the dominant tree species since the Ice Age.

Pine by Martin Klatt.

Juniper

Cypress family: *Cupressaceae*
Common Juniper *(Juniperus communis)*

Physical appearance

Junipers are evergreen shrubs or small trees with needle-like, rigid, spiky leaves, and globular cones covered in touching scales. The cones of all junipers are fleshy and appear as berries, which, however, they are not in the botanical sense. While very tall trees can be found among other members of cypress family, most junipers are rather small, apart from some Asian species, and the Pencil Cedar *(Juniperus virginiana)*, a narrow, pyramid-shaped tree native to eastern and central North America.

The Common Juniper is the most widely spread conifer on Earth and can be found anywhere in the northern hemisphere. It is usually multi-stemmed, and rarely higher than 10 m (30 feet). The young shoots are triangular in shape, and the spiny leaves, arranged in whorls of three, are grey-green with a broad white band above. Juniper occurs in a wide variety of shapes, but its typical one is a slender column or broad and irregularly conical.

The male and female cones are found on separate trees. The males are small and yellow; the females are fleshy, green and globular. The berry-like fruit are initially green but ripen blue-black within three years. The flesh is dry, resinous, and very aromatic and usually contains three seeds. Mice, other rodents and birds eat the seeds and spread them over a wide area.

Juniper has deep roots that can adapt to almost any soil, whether chalky, rich in humus, poor and sandy, rocky or even acidic moorland, for example, Dwarf Juniper. It even ventures beyond the tree line in the Alps, up to altitudes of 3,000 m (10,000 feet). Juniper only avoids badly drained soil. Heat, cold and other extremes do not pose problems for the tree, but it does need direct light.

Its toughness and adaptability make it a very powerful pioneer tree, and it was one of the first trees to return to the barren tundra after the Ice Age.

Above: Juniper by Per-Olaf Mademann.   *Below: Juniper by Martin Klatt.*

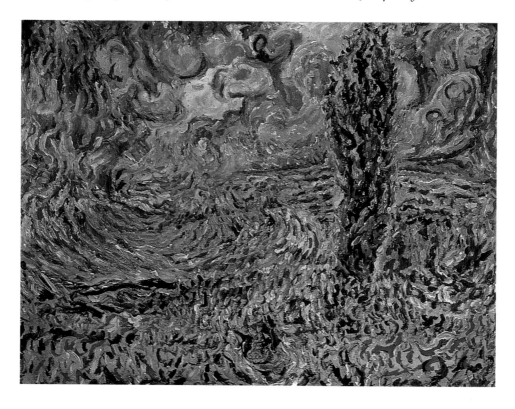

Juniper grove by Martin Klatt.

Juniper is a tree of enormous vitality; its branches can take root, and the trunk can also produce new shoots. Its adaptability allows it to dominate meagre stands, but it has to give way in dense woodland.

All in all, Juniper displays a mixture of vitality, perseverance and regenerative power and restraint and slow growth. Juniper sacrifices height for survival in harsh and extreme conditions.

Healing

Juniper 'berries' — with the exception of the poisonous Stinking Juniper *(Juniperus foetidissima)*, which is native to the Mediterranean — play an important role in healing. They are diuretic, disinfectant, warming and generally toning, and stimulate circulation and the whole metabolism. Eating one fresh or dried berry a day is a good boost for the body's immune system. Early herbalists regarded Juniper as a strong antidote to the plague.

Its diuretic effect is mainly due to essential oils, which stimulate the kidney tissues. Juniper fruits help to treat bladder problems, rheumatism, gout, coughs, asthma and skin diseases. They strengthen the nervous system and stimulate appetite and digestion. For a juniper *cure*, three 'berries' can be chewed on day one, increasing the number daily by one up to fifteen berries, then decreasing the amount in the same way, back to three. Juniper water can be drunk instead. Leave two teaspoons of 'berries' for eight hours in a jug containing two glasses of cold water. This is then strained and drunk during the day. Externally, juniper can be used as a wash for skin infections, in ointments, and as a cleansing incense (see below).

An overdose of juniper fruits may irritate the kidneys, and the above amounts should, therefore, not be exceeded. Juniper is not recommended during pregnancy or for people with kidney disorders.

The most common use of Juniper 'berries' is for flavouring gin. Worldwide, Juniper berries were also commonly used as a contraceptive, as the acidic juice from the fruits, when applied to the relevant parts of the body, killed sperm. However, eventually, the Church started destroying the trees after noticing falling birth rates!

Tradition

Most European names for this tree are derived from Latin *juniperus;* a term believed to stem from *junior* (the younger), and *parere* (to appear), which relates to the fact that the younger, green fruits appear while the previous ones are still maturing. The German *Wacholder* is even more interesting since it derives from Old High German *wachaltar,* from *wehhal, wachal* (awake, fresh), and *tar* (tree).

This 'awake tree' enjoyed much veneration from the people. According to an old German saying one should take one's hat off when passing either Juniper or Elder. An Austrian saying states: 'For Elder and Juniper I remove my hat and make a half-bow,' whereas in Switzerland they said: 'For Elder we shall take off our hats, and for Juniper we shall bend our knees.'

This respect is probably due to its benevolent effects for cleansing the body and the house (see above). The smoke has also been used for healing people or protecting animals. Juniper wood was carved into protective talismans and wands, and the twigs were believed to give protection against any bad spirits or the 'evil eye' (Fife 1994).

In the British Isles, juniper twigs were hung above doorways at Beltane, and burnt at Samhain (Milner 1992), as well as amongst Slavic, Finno-Ugric and Baltic peoples. A Chinese report mentions Tibetan healers treating patients with Juniper smoke (Stäubli 1927, 8). The widespread use of Juniper for cleansing with its smoke was so important that in many German and Swiss dialects the trees had a second name — *Räucholder, Racholder,*

Reckolder — from the German *Rauch* meaning 'smoke.' In Germany, the parents of an ill child took an offering of wool and bread to a Juniper tree, speaking the words: 'You blessed ones, here I bring you something to spin, and something to eat, for the healing of our child.'

In Scotland at Samhain (All Souls Night), when the gates to the Realm of the Dead were believed to be more open than at any other time of the year, people would burn some juniper on their doorstep, to keep unwanted spirits away from the house. Furthermore, the word *Samhain* seems to be closely related to one of the Gallic names for Juniper, *samh*.

The Brothers Grimm recorded another connection between Juniper and death. In the story *The Juniper Tree,* the soul of a dead child rises like a bird from a mist emanating from a juniper. Various tales refer to Juniper as the entrance to the dwellings of giants or dwarfs, or to the underworld. In Bavaria and Bohemia it was also one of the trees giving the Life Rod.

Inspiration

It is surprising how many gifts this small, dark conifer gives to people as well as to its environment. Juniper's most typical habitats are barren and rather empty, like rocky hill slopes or wide open moorland where maybe some Birch and Pine enrich the scenery, but not much else. Like Larch, Juniper combines many powers and aspects, for the wholeness of its natural habitat, as well as for the soul of the local people.

Juniper was the Life Rod and fertility symbol. It protected children, adults and animals alike, and kept unwanted influences and spirits at bay. It was also used on Germanic funeral pyres and in Greek rituals dedicated to Hecate, goddess of the underworld.

Yew

Yew family: *Taxaceae*
Common Yew *(Taxus baccata)*

Physical appearance

Yew is a dense evergreen tree, which is conical or domed in shape. It is rarely of great height but has a massive trunk. It is found in the Himalayas, Europe and North America. It thrives on rich soil, particularly lime, but generally grows on any soil. It is a tree often seen in shady locations, but can also be found free-standing, although a tree does have difficulty if suddenly exposed to direct light, forcing it to adapt in a hurry. Yew tends to be multi-stemmed and has a crown of dark green, needle-like leaves, which contrasts its reddish bark and scarlet berry-like fruits (arils) in the autumn. The multi-layered bark of older branches peels off in oblong flakes, creating patterns of red-brown hues. The leaves are flat and rather soft and are spirally placed on long shoots on alternate sides of short shoots. They are glossy and dark green on top, and yellowish green underneath, and waxy like the needles of all conifers. However, the tree is non-resinous. All parts of the Yew, apart from the red arils, are poisonous.

The Irish Yew *(Taxus baccata* var. *fastigiata)* with its cypress-like appearance is a variety that was discovered on the slopes of Cuilcagh Mountain, County Fermanagh, between 1740 and 1760. It can only be propagated from the suckers of existing trees.

While conifers are usually hermaphrodite, yews are either male or female, although bisexual trees do exist. The yellow male flowers are small, globular structures sitting singly on the leaf axils beneath the previous year's branches. Female flowers are located in similar positions; they are tiny and green, and swell after pollination. A hard, dark green seed is surrounded by the cup-like aril, which is open at the top. Initially green, the arils become fleshy and sweet, and later bright scarlet. The seeds are propagated by the many birds which feed on the non-toxic arils.

Yew is a very vital tree. In Britain its pollen count is one of the highest, despite the relative scarcity of the tree. Its trunk can easily produce new

Yew aril.

shoots after being cut down or storm-damaged, and root suckers are an additional, effective way of reproducing. However, Yew has a third way of reproducing, called *layering,* which is very rare among non-tropical plants. A branch of any size grows towards the ground and takes root. The original intention is to support the spreading limbs of the existing trunk, but this new root also produces young, upright, growing shoots and eventually can become a new tree. People talk about *young* trees but it is, in fact, all one tree, not a mass of separate beings. Thus a ring or grove of new trees can surround the mother tree. This process is very rare and can be seen at Ormeston in East Lothian, in a remote, overgrown part of the grounds of Ormeston Hall, near to a ruined chapel, and at Newlands Corner, in Surrey, a mixed Oak-woodland on the north downs of chalk hills, where several Yew specimens can be found.

The most astonishing qualities of Yew are its slow growth, which gives Yew incredible longevity, and its enormous regenerative power, which allows the tree to sprout again, even after a total loss of its crown. Yews have hard, durable wood and, together with boxwood, is the hardest wood of the European temperate zone.

While the heartwood inside the hollowing trunk slowly rots away sheaths of new growth encase the old dead wood, to strengthen and protect it. Thus Yew renews itself from the outside in. The cambium growth keeps up with the rate of decay; at a pace of about 2.5 cm (1 inch) increase in girth every twenty-five years. However, in the temperate zone, the average for solitary trees is 2.5 cm (1″) per *year*. A yew that appears to be a hollow, decaying wreck is often at the beginning of its self-regeneration process. Yew can *resurrect* itself from complete decay. There is no biological reason for a yew tree to die — it can virtually live forever.

As a result, no piece of wood on an old yew is as old as the whole tree, a fact that makes carbon dating impossible. There are no tree rings to count either, so for a long time, the age of yew trees was wrongly calculated. Until the 1980s, botanists commonly thought that Yew hardly ever exceeded eight hundred years of age. This opinion changed in 1988, following the publication of detailed research by Allen Meredith, backed up by Alan Mitchell, one of Britain's leading tree experts, and David Bellamy, the well-known British botanist. In Tandridge, Surrey, Allen Meredith discovered an ancient yew tree about eight metres (25 feet) from the church, which has Saxon foundations. In the crypt, stone vaulting is clearly visible, which was constructed by Saxon builders around the tree's roots. Yew trees do not increase in height after reaching maturity, and their roots increase very slowly in diameter. These findings not only show the respect Saxon Christians had for the tree, but also indicate that this tree was fully grown when the church was built — a thousand years ago! This piece of evidence finally swayed others (Cheton & Bruton 1994, 47). The Yew's age is now believed to be in excess of 2,500 years.

Since Allen Meredith's original research in the 1970s and 80s, the number of recognised ancient yews has increased constantly. In the winter of 2005/2006, the database of the Ancient Yew Group (AYG), an independent research group in Britain, held more than 800 entries for yews considered to be older than 500 years. A full listing of the British locations of ancient yew trees, including their measurements, history and current state can be found on the AYG's website (www.ancient-yew.org.uk). The oldest yew trees are estimated to be between 2,000 and 3,000 years old, though some are believed to be as much as 5,000 years old or more. However, it is commonly agreed that the oldest yew tree is at Fortingall (Tayside) in Scotland. Estimates for its age vary from 3,000 to 8,000 years, but it is certainly one of the oldest trees in the world, and could even be the oldest (Chetan & Bruton 1994, 25f; Bellamy, *The Times*, 3 October, 1998). However, you will still not find it in the record books at present, because many scientists still rely on tree rings to age a tree, which keeps the Great Basin Bristlecone Pine *(Pinus longeava)* at the top of the list, followed by Redwood *(Sequoia giganteum)*.

David Bellamy gives a rough guide for estimating the age of a yew by measuring its girth, which should always be measured 1.5 m (5 feet) from the ground. Very young trees may increase their girth by 12 mm (0.5") each year, and one thousand-year-old trees only by about 3 mm (0.125") a year. After this age, the growth rate sinks below one millimetre, and single trees have been measured whose girth even decreased over decades.

However, any yew tree might be even older, since aerial roots can also grow inside the hollow trunk — there are fifteen living examples of this in England and Wales — and might one day entirely replace the existing tree. A visible yew tree might not be the first *body* of an ancient root. The lifespan of Yew is dictated more by climate shifts, ice ages and geological events than by botanical laws.

With its outstanding adaptability and regenerative powers, Yew is one of the oldest and most successful species. Yew fossils that have been found,

The Yew at Linton, Herefordshire,   *The Yew at Tandridge, Surrey, England.*
England.

and believed to be one million years old, are virtually indistinguishable from the tree we know today. Yews were common in the Neolithic, the Bronze, and the Iron Ages, and only became less prevalent because of man's activities. During the Middle Ages, as the Yew's strong and flexible wood became the first choice for bows and longbows, a catastrophic decline began. In 1369, the English king, Edward III, decreed that archery practice be compulsory for every able-bodied man. On the continent yew bows were also in high demand. By 1492, England had to start importing yew wood, and parliament decreed that every trading ship, which unloaded in an English harbour, had to bring back four yew bows per ton of freight.

This practice resulted in the death of countless continental yews, which were particularly abundant in the Alps. After the export of between six hundred thousand and one million yew bows from Bavaria and Austria within five decades, there were no yew trees left in Bavaria by 1568. For these reasons nearly all of the ancient yews remaining today are found in churchyards.

In Britain, between the world wars there were still more than one thousand yews of more than one thousand years of age. Since then the number has decreased by more than half. This is partly due to storm damage, but most have been needlessly felled, because people did not know that a decaying, rotten tree was about to start a new lease of life.

Healing

Every part of the Yew tree is poisonous, apart from the red aril around the (also poisonous) seed, and it is the only toxic conifer in Europe. Some wild animals feed on Yew, particularly deer who receive some kind of 'kick' from the yew's alkaloids (nitrogen compounds), but it is fatal to domestic animals and humans. Unfortunately, horses like to eat yew sprays, with tragic results. 0.2–0.3 g of yew leaves per kilogram of body weight is regarded as a fatal amount for a horse; about one gram per kilogram of body weight is fatal for humans, or three to five fruit stones. Children under five are even more sensitive.

The leaves are the most toxic part of the tree; the lowest alkaloid concentration in the leaves appears in May, the highest in the autumn and in January. The alkaloid, *taxicantin*, causes palpitations and breathing difficulties, and within a few hours, paralysis, coma and heart failure. It also induces contractions of the womb, and was used as an abortifacient in post-medieval times, often killing the mother as well. Caesar reported that, when defeated, the chief of the People of the Yew took his own life

Inside the hollow trunk of the Yew at Linton.

with the help of yew poison. Some also believe that some Celts and Teutons poisoned their arrowheads with taxicantin. The Greeks and Romans certainly did.

Although poisonous in certain quantities, in minute quantities Yew can be a cardiac tonic. In India, the leaves are used as a stomach medicine, and to treat rheumatism. Native Americans used yew as an anti-inflammatory agent (Chetan & Bruton 1994, 234).

In Western medicine, Yew came to sudden fame in cancer therapy. Between 1960 and 1981, more than 114,000 plant extracts and more than 16,000 animal extracts were tested for anti-cancerous properties. Only one was both effective and safe: *taxol*, derived from the yew tree. Tests showed promising results — particularly for cancer of the ovaries, breasts and lungs. After 1988, demand for the Pacific Yew *(Taxus brevifolia)*, native to North America, increased, but taxol is only found in small amounts, and the treatment of one patient requires the life of six trees a year. Vast nurseries have been established in California and, luckily, research into the synthetic production of taxol seems to be having positive results.

Tradition

Yew has been of major spiritual significance to humankind from the earliest times. Many Christian churchyards are located on much older sacred sites, and quite a few Celtic or Germanic sanctuaries reach even further back, to the Bronze or even the Stone Age. Many of these sites have burial mounds inside a round enclosure, and a good number of ancient churchyards in England and Wales are still either slightly higher than the surroundings, or round, or both; for example, Llanelly and Discoed. The church at Llanfihangel-nant-Melan, Wales is still surrounded by a circle of hollow yews (around 1,800 years old), and some others have remnants of sacred circles.

Nearly all yews with a girth of over 6.6 m (22 feet) are older than the stone church next to them. In England, the Norman Conquest in the eleventh century, brought rectangular churchyards, in some of which new yews were planted in each corner.

Yews were sacred centres of tribal territories. Fortingall (where the oldest yew stands) is not only near the geographical centre of Scotland, but is also an ancient site with a Bronze Age tumulus (burial mound) known as *Carn nam Marbh*, the Mound of the Dead. There is no doubt that the yew trees at sacred sites have been consciously planted by people. Fortingall, and nearly all of the other remaining yews exceeding four thousand years of age, are found to the north of the circular tumulus. For reasons unknown to us, the people of the Megalithic culture who built Newgrange, Stonehenge and Avebury wanted yew trees to the north of their burial mounds.

Between 3500 and 3000 BC the orientation of the yews changed to an east-west axis through the centre of the tumulus, and this remained a characteristic of Celtic sites as well. When the Anglo-Saxons came to Britain they planted yews at sacred sites as well, but mainly on the south side.

The world's oldest man-made wooden artefact is a yew spear found in Clacton, Essex, which dates from about 150,000 years ago. Another yew spear, about 90,000 years old, was found between the ribs of a straight-tusked mammoth in Lower Saxony. The oldest English yew bow (from 2600 BC) was found on the Somerset levels, and the 5,300-year-old 'Iceman' discovered on the Italian-Austrian border, had a yew longbow measuring 1.8 m (6 feet), although he himself was only 1.55 m (5 ft 2") tall (Chetan & Bruton 1994, 78; Milner 1992; Wilkinson 1981, 24; Graupe 1991). Although none of these items offer any evidence of the spiritual meaning of the tree, the mythical Norse god, Ullr, the divine archer who lives in *Yew Valley*, certainly indicates the link between weapons and their spiritual significance.

All Germanic tribes had a rich lore based around the Yew. A rune was dedicated to it — *Ihwaz* or *eiwaz* is the thirteenth rune, and generally believed to represent death and rebirth. Younger Scandinavian runes even have a second sign for Yew, *yr*, which represents the roots of the Tree of Life (see Hageneder, *The Heritage of Trees*). In an Old Norse song, the Yew is called *vetrgrønstr vida* (wintergreenest tree), and it is governed by Ullr, whose bow is believed to be the rune, *ur*, with the shape of the mother mound of midwinter (Wirth 1979, 462). Thus Graves was right, when he assigned Yew to the midwinter solstice in his tree calendar. Wirth also assigned Yew to the south *(yr)* and particularly to the north *(eiwaz)*, decades before the true age of the British churchyard yews was revealed, and before the discovery that the Anglo-Saxons had planted their sacred Yews in exactly the same way.

Various yew wood talismans have been excavated, particularly on various Frisian Islands, where the climate has helped to preserve them. One is

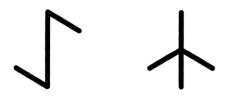

The Germanic runes of yr *and* eiwaz.

a small seventh-century amulet with the runic inscription 'Always carry this yew! Therein lies strength!' Another is an early ninth-century yew wand from Holland, with a carved invocation in Anglo-Saxon runes, to calm the waves of the sea.

Yggdrasil, the Germanic World Tree is a yew. The Old Norse *barraskr* denotes 'needle-ash,' and it is described as evergreen. However, the Ash bears no needles nor is it evergreen. Odin — the archetype of the shaman searching for knowledge — sacrifices one of his eyes in his search for knowledge, and is closely associated with the World Tree. An Odin figure, probably an offering to water, was excavated in Britain, and is made of yew wood (Coles 1998, 168). It is astonishing that a one-eyed Odin figure dating from the eleventh century BC, has been found in Britain, since there is no record of such an early Germanic invasion of the British Isles. This find then implies that the worship of a one-eyed shaman figure might be much older than first assumed, and was not necessarily exclusively Germanic in origin.

The drink made from the sap of the Tree of Knowledge is the drink from the mythical cauldron of inspiration. As Nigel Pennick points out, the yew rune has the shape of the pot-hook holding a cauldron over the cooking fire (Pennick 1992, 79–81). The World Tree is the structure that holds the cauldron in which all life *boils*. Since Yew holds the worlds together, its hard wood was also perfect for making the nails for Viking ships.

It seems that yew lore has a common Indo-European heritage. One of its old Indian names, *deodaru*, means 'tree of god' or 'divine tree.' Today, *Deodar* is the name of a Himalayan cedar (*Cedrus deodara*). In Hindu culture, the traditional paint for the *bindhi*, the dot on the forehead, was originally made from powdered yew bark, and marks the point of the *third eye,* an energy point stimulating higher perception and understanding. Future research will have reveal if Yew bears any links with the legendary Indian soma, the 'drink of the gods.' It is quite possible that ancient Indian sages knew how to prepare a mind-altering potion from the alkaloids of this tree, comparable to *soma*, the drink of the Indian gods.

In ancient Celtic culture Yew was also associated with higher knowledge and wisdom. It was the principal wood for carving ogham runes, the signs of the tree alphabet. Scottish Druids used yew staffs with notches or *oghams* to record the phases of the moon or the traditional laws (Fife 1994). The Irish word for salmon (see Hazel, the Salmon of Wisdom) is *eo*, the same as the word for Yew (Chetan & Bruton 1994, 226).

Some Celtic tribes named themselves after the Yew tree, for instance, the *Eburones*, the *Esuvii* and the *Eburomagus*. One Swiss settlement was called *Eburodun*. Ireland really means 'Yew Island;' the Greeks and Romans called it *Ierne* called it *Ierne* and *Iubernia* respectively (Chetan & Bruton 1994).

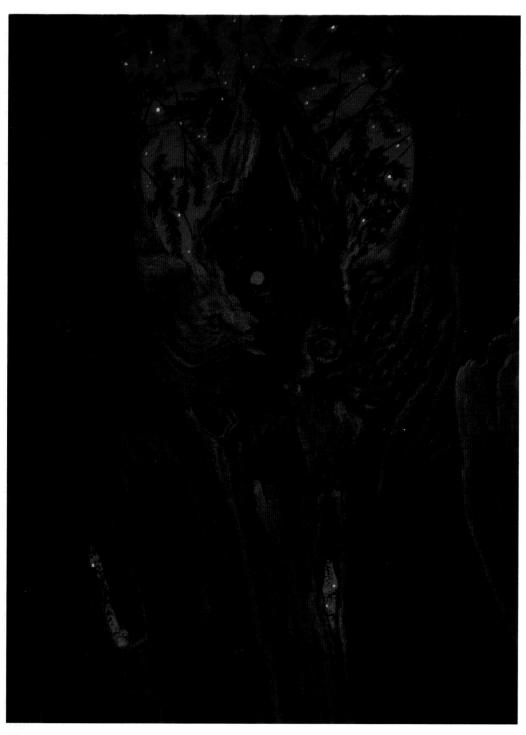

Yew.

The five sacred trees of Ireland were said to have grown from berries from a single branch, and this could only have come from Yew. The central significance of the Yew for Celtic Ireland — the Yew Island — is revealed by the lore around Danu, the great mother goddess, and her descendants. Danu (also called Dana, Aine, Ana or Anu) was the ancestral mother of the *fir sidhe* or *Tuatha Dé Danann*. She gave birth to three sons who were Yew trees. She nursed the *fir sidhe* or *Tuatha Dé Danann,* who in Irish myth are revered as gods and goddesses, and she was the daughter of the Dagda, the good god, himself, who is closely associated with the magical cauldron.

The sacred hill, *Cnoc Aine,* in Munster, is dedicated to Danu and contains the mythic genealogy of the kings of Ireland. The three mounds and two cairns on the top are consecrated to Danu (Aine) herself, to two of her sons, Uainide and Eogabal, to her father, and to her brother, *Fer hI* (Dames 1996, 63). The names of the two brothers denote 'green foliage' and 'a crotch or fork in a Yew tree' respectively. *Fer hI* means 'Man of Yew.' It is therefore reasonable to expect that Danu, too, must have been seen as a Yew. Celtic invaders respected this family of Yew children as the first race of the Yew Island. The dynasty that ruled Munster from the seventh to the tenth century AD, was called the *Eoganacht,* obviously gaining political right for their rule by association with the Yew (Chetan & Bruton 1994, 224).

The Irish tale of *The Yew Tree of the Disputing Sons (Dindshenchas)* tells how the mortal hero, Ailill, and his sons carelessly allow their horses to graze in the domain of the *sidhe* (a yew grove). In the arising dispute Eogabul and Danu (Aine) — Yew fork and Danu herself — are killed. The surviving *Fer hI* decides to teach the humans a lesson and creates a yew tree of incredible beauty, which causes the culprits to quarrel and destroy each other over possession of the tree. This family of Yew children, who so easily create a new yew tree, are thus deities of an ancient yew grove.

Bardic language often referred to yew berries as either *nuts* (the hard green fruits), *acorns* (because they sit in small cups) or *apples* (red fruits were often called 'apples' in the past). This has caused much confusion in mythology. Although Avalon is certainly derived from the word for apple, orchards were not the only magical element of ancient Glastonbury. Celtic *tan* means red, fire (as in Beltane), and *tann* means 'sacred tree' (originally denoting Yew, the red tree), while *glas* is '(ever)green.' Glastonbury is named after an *(ever)green sacred tree,* and excavations around the well have revealed the stump of a yew tree at a depth of 3.6 m (11ft 9") (Chetan & Bruton 1994, 160). Whatever the role of *apples* at Glastonbury, it is rather difficult to imagine the passage of King Arthur without Yew being involved.

Many of the Irish Christian saints started to preach under ancient sacred yews, or even lived in the hollow tree. In medieval Celtic stories, Yew often features in connection with lovers. King Conchobar tries to separate the graves of Deirdre and Naoise with yew stakes, but they grow into trees weaving their branches together and uniting the lovers even in death. Similarly, Tristan and Iseult are buried on either side of a chapel but the yew trees on their graves eventually intertwine above the chapel roof. Countless customs and stories from the Christian era refer to Yew as the graveyard tree of the Celtic west. In Wales, for example, it is called 'the gentle guardian of the dead' (Trevelyan 1909, 102).

Inspiration

Megalithic sites like Stonehenge are remarkable to us for their antiquity. Nearly all ancient sites are of stone, but some yew trees are *living* beings of equal age. The yew tree at Discoed in Wales was possibly already about five hundred years old when the first stones from the Presceli mountains passed it on their way to Stonehenge — and the tree is still alive!

We are able to understand more of the significance that Yew held for the people of the past when we comprehend the meaning of these ancient burial mounds. Before Christianity, death was perceived as a transition in a long life. For the ancients: 'the boundary between the worlds of the dead and the living was not real. The dead continued invisibly and were present at all important occasions' *(Encyclopaedia Britannica)*. In order to invite the dead to a ceremony, the living would go to the tumulus, which was the meeting point of the worlds. In the sacred circle death is just a part of perpetual life; nature displays this everywhere. Yew represents the unity of life and death. In Western societies the suppression of the deeper understanding of death led to the distorted image of Yew as the 'tree of death.' However, Yew actually practises resurrection, and, if anything, Yew is the 'tree of life.'

Like the old Irish tree circles, the trees of any region on Earth can be conceived as a sacred circle of sublime spirits, each of whom hold special physical and spiritual gifts for its local ecology as well as for the human race. However, Yew is not part of the wheel, it is everything around it! One's guide in death can be the Elder mother, but eventually she will deliver you to a region beyond time and, on Earth, this energy expresses itself as Yew. Yew is eternity.

The German word for eternity, *Ewigkeit*, (Old High German, *ewa, ewi*) derives from the ancient name for Yew (Old High German, *iwe, iwa*). The Celtic names for the yew tree are based on the *'ee'* sound, for example the Breton *iuin;* Welsh *ywen;* Gallic *iubhar;* Gaelic *iúr;* and Old Irish *idhadh* and *eo.* Anglo-Saxon pronunciations vary between *ie, eo, y* and *e,* according to dialect. The Anglo-Saxon *eo* is especially noteworthy because of its similarity to the Old High German *eo, io* meaning 'always, eternally,' and the fact that the Anglo-Saxon language has its roots in Old High German. The Old Irish *eo* means 'yew' (Wirth, 1979,160; Kluge, 1975, 177). Thus there are many links between the yew's name and words for eternity.

In sound therapy (or singing), the *'ee'* sound is the one that resonates most strongly in the head. In Celtic and Germanic languages various words for Yew and self-consciousness are therefore closely linked. The Anglo-Saxon *ih* denotes both 'I' and 'Yew,' and the Norse name for Yew as the World Tree, *Ygg-drasil,* means 'I-carrier,' 'carrier of the I.'

In the Old Testament Ezekiel says that the Tree of Life and all the trees of Eden have come down with us into the abyss (of physical reality). The trees of paradise manifest themselves as the trees of any local tree circle, and the Tree of Life and Knowledge takes the shape of Yew.

A gateway of trees.

A beech branch.

Afterword

By taking a deep look at the myths, legends, folklore and customs surrounding trees we can see how trees have inspired and nourished the human soul since the dawn of history. Ezekiel said that 'the trees of Eden' will be brought down to 'the nether world' (31:18), to help us unite all levels of reality, both spiritual and material. In the Book of Revelation, John says: '... the leaves of the trees were for the healing of the nations,' (22:2). All cultures have venerated trees for their practical, as well as spiritual, gifts. This is discussed in further detail in *The Heritage of Trees*.

Trees are vital for the survival of all life forms on Earth. If the last extensive woodlands, whether tropical or temperate, are destroyed, Earth will become uninhabitable. Trees and humans stand and fall together.

Despite the worrying statistics of biodiversity loss, a keen interest in, and compassion for, other life forms is the only effective way of inspiring people to care about endangered parts of creation. Historically, man has only fought for something he knows intimately, which has been the ecological legacy of myth and religion. I hope that *The Spirit of Trees* makes a positive contribution towards reuniting these elements in the twenty-first century.

Etymological Appendix

Abbreviations:

AS   Anglo-Saxon
Bret.   Breton
Gael.   Gaelic
Lat.   Latin
ME   Middle English
Norw,   Norwegian
OE   Old English
OGerm. Old Germanic
OHG   Old High German
OIr.   Old Irish
ON   Old Norse
Sc.-Gael Scots Gaelic

Birch

OE. *bierce, birce*, AS. *birce*, Viking *birk*, OHG. *birka*,
Bret. *bezo*, Welsh *bedwen*, Sc.-Gael. *beithe*, Gael. *beith gheal*, OIr. *beithe*

Rowan

from Norw. *rogn, raun*, Icel. *reynir*, OHG. *eberboum*,
Bret. *kerzinenn*, Welsh *criafol*, Sc.-Gael. *caorann*, Gael. *caorthann*, OIr. *luis*

Ash

OE. *æsc, aes*, AS., ON. *askr*, OHG. *ask*, OGerm. *ask-oz*,
Bret. *onn*, Welsh *onnen*, Sc.-Gael. *uinnsean*, Gael. *fuinseog*, OIr. *nion*, Gaul. *onna*

Alder

OE. *alor, aler*, AS. *alor, aler*, Goth *alisa*, Old Prussian *alskande*, ON. *elri*, OHG. *erila*,
    OGerm. *Alisa, alizo*,
Bret. *gwern*, Welsh *gwernen*, Sc.-Gael. *fearn*, Gael. *fearnóg*, OIr. *fearn*

Willow

OE. *welig*, AS. *welig, wipig, sealh* (Sallow), Icel. *vidir*, OHG. *wida*,
Bret. *haleg*, Welsh *helygen*, Sc.-Gael. *seileach*, Gael. *saileach*, OIr. *sail*

Poplar

OE. *popler* from Old French *poplier*, OHG. *albari*,
Bret. *haleg*, Welsh *polysen*, Gael. *poibleog*

Aspen

OE. *aespe*, AS. *æsp*, ON. *asp*, OHG. *aspa*,
Bret. *elf-krenerez*, Welsh *polysen wen, aethnen*, Sc.-Gael. *critheann*, Gael. *crann creathach*, OIr. *eadhadh*

Hawthorn

OE. *hagg*, AS. *hæthorn*,
Bret. *spern-gwenn*, Welsh *draenen wen*, Sc.-Gael. *sgitheach*, Gael. *sceach (gheal)*, OIr. *Huath*

Maple

OE. *mapel, mapul*, AS. *mapuldor*, OGerm. *maplo-*, related to OHG. *mazzaltra* (= juniper), *linboum*,
Bret. *skao-gwrac'h gwenn*, Welsh *sycamorwydden*, Gael. *Seiceamar*

Elm

OE. *elm*, AS. *elm, wice*, ON. *almr*, OHG. *ëlm, ilme, elmaha*, Teutonic *elmo-z*,
Bret. *evlec'h*, Welsh *llwyfen*, Sc.-Gael. *leamhan*, Gael. *leamhán*, OIr. *lem*

Beech

OE. *bece*, AS. *bōk, bece*, OHG. *buohha*, MHG. *buoche*,
Bret. *fao*, Welsh *ffawydden*, Sc.-Gael. *faidbhile*, Gael. *fáibhile (bhile*, sacred tree)

Oak

OE. *ak*, AS. *æ-c, a-c*, ON. *eik*, OHG. *eih*, Teutonic *aiks*,
Bret. *derv*, Welsh *derwen*, Sc.-Gael. *darach*, Gael. *dair*, OIr. *duir*

Holly

OE. *holegn*, ME *holin*, AS. *holen*, OHG. *hul(i)s*,
Bret. *kelenn*, Welsh *celynnen*, Sc.-Gael. *cuilleann*, Gael. *cuileann*, OIr. *tinne*

Hazel

OE. *hæsel*, AS. *hæsel, hæsl*, ON. *hasl*, OHG. *hasal* (masc.), *hasala* (fem.), OGerm. *hasalo-z*,
Bret. *kraonkelvezenn*, Welsh *collen*, Sc.-Gael. *calltainn*, Gael. *coll*, OIr. *coll*

Apple

OE. *æppel*, AS. *apuldor, æppeltréow*, OGerm. *æppel*, ON. *apaldr, epli*, OHG. *aphol, apfal*,
Bret. *avalenn*, Welsh *afallen*, Sc.-Gael. *abhall*, Gael. *úll*, OIr. *queirt*

Ivy

OE. *ifig,* AS. *ifig,* OHG. *ëbah,*
Bret. *i, io,* Welsh *eiddew, iorwg,* Sc.-Gael. *eidheann,* Gael. *eidhneán,* OIr. *gort*

Blackthorn

OE. *blace thyrne,* AS. *slahthorn,* OHG. *sleha, slewa,*
Bret. *irinenn,* Welsh *draenen ddu,* Sc.-Gael. *droigheann,* Gael. *draighean,* OIr. *straiph*

Elder

OE. *ellaern,* AS. *ellen,* OHG. *holuntar, holantar,*
Bret. *skao,* Welsh *ysgawen,* Sc.-Gael. *droman,* Gael. *trom,* OIr. *ruis*

Lime (Linden)

altered form of OE. *line, linden,* AS. *linde, bæst,* OHG. *linta,*
Bret. *tilh,* Welsh *palalwyfen,* Sc.-Gael. *teile,* Gael. *teile*

Fir

OE. *fyre,* OGerm. *furhjôn, forhâ,* ON. *fyri* (fir), OHG. *fiotha, forha,*
Bret. *sapr,* Welsh *ffynidwydden,* Sc.-Gael. *giuthas* (Lochlannach), Gael. *giúis,* OIr. *ailm*

Larch

Lat. *larix* is of Celtic origin, OHG. *larihha, lerihha,*

Pine

OE. *pîn,* OS *pîna,* OHG. *kienforha,*
Bret. *pin,* Welsh *pinwydden,* Sc.-Gael. *giuthas,* Gael. *crann péine*

Juniper

AS. *cvicbeám,* OHG. *quëkholter, wachaltar,*
Bret. *jenevra,* Welsh *merywen,* Sc.-Gael. *aiteann,* Gael. *aiteal*

Yew

OE. *iw, eow,* AS. *ich, ioh,* ON. *yr,* OHG. *iwa, iha,* OGerm. *ivo,* Suisse *iche, ige,*
Bret. *iuin,* Welsh *ywen,* Sc.-Gael. *iubhar,* Gael. *iúr,* OIr. *idhadh*

Bibliography

Quotes from German sources have been translated by the author.

Alexandersson, Olof, *Living Water,* Gateway Books, 1990.

Amber, Reuben, *Color Therapy,* Aurora Press, Santa Fe 1983.

Arndt, Ulrich, 'Geheimnisse des Wassers' in *Esotera* 8/1996, Freiburg 1996.

Bischof, Marco, *Biophotonen: Das Licht in unseren Zellen, Zweitausendeins,* Frankfurt 1995.

Black Book of Carmarthen, see Pennar

Bötticher, Carl, *Der Baumkultus der Hellenen*, Berlin 1856.

Bracegirdle, Brian, & Miles, Patricia H., *An Atlas of Plant Structure,* Heinneman Educational Books 1971.

Brasier, Clive, *New Horizons in Dutch Elm Disease Control,* Forestry Commission, Edinburgh, 1996.

Caldecott, Moyra, *Myths of the Sacred Tree,* Destiny, Rochester, Vermont 1993.

Calder, George (Ed.), *Auraicept na n-Éces* (The Scholar's Primer), Edinburgh 1917.

Car-Gomm, Philip, *The Elements of the Druid Tradition,* Element Books, Shaftesbury 1991.

Caro, Paul, *Water*, McGraw-Hill, New York 1993.

Chadwick, Nora, *The Celts*, Penguin, 1991.

Chalmers, J.A., *Journal for Atmospheric and Terrestrial Physic,* No. 3/1953, 346f

— *Journal for Atmospheric and Terrestrial Physic,* No. 6/1955, 149–59.

Chetan, Anand & Bruton, Diana, *The Sacred Yew,* Arkana, 1994.

Cleasby, Richard & Vigfusson, Gudbrand, *An Icelandic-English Dictionary,* Oxford University Press, 1975.

Coats, Callum (Transl. & Ed.), *The Water Wizard*: *The Extraordinary Properties of Natural Water, Viktor Schauberger,* Gateway Books, 1997.

Coles, Bryony, 'Anthropomorphic Wooden Figures from Britain and Ireland,' in Gibson, Burl & Simpson.

Coles, Bryony, 'Wood Species for Wooden Figures: A Glimpse of a Pattern,' in *Prehistoric Ritual and Religion,* Sutton, Stroud 1998

Cook, Roger, *The Tree of Life: Image of the Cosmos,* Thames & Hudson, 1992.

Cousens, John, *An Introduction to Woodland Ecology,* Oliver & Boyd, 1974.

Cuncliffe, Barry (Ed.), *The Oxford Illustrated Prehistory of Europe,* Oxford University Press, 1994.

Dames, Michael, *Mythic Ireland,* Thames & Hudson, 1996.

Davies, Jonathan Ceredig, *Folk-Lore of West and Mid-Wales,* Aberystwyth, 1911.

Devlin, Robert M. & Witham, Francis H., *Plant Physiology,* Wadsworth Publishing Company, California 1983.

Diederichs, Ulf (Ed.), (Transl. by Felix Genzmer, Gustav Neckel) *Germanische Götterlehre: Nach den Quellen der Lieder und Prosa-Edda,* Diederichs, Cologne 1984.

Dimitri, L., Rajda, V., 'The electro-diagnostic as a new method to determine the vitality of trees,' in *Forstw. Cbl.* 114, Blackwell Wissenschafts Verlag, Berlin 1995.

Earwood, Caroline, *Domestic Wooden Artefacts in Britain and Ireland from Neolithic to Viking times,* University of Exeter Press, 1993.

Edwards, Lawrence, *The Vortex of Life,* Floris Books, 1993.

Faulkner, R.O., *The Ancient Egyptian Book of the Dead,* British Museum Publications, 1985.

Fife, Hugh, *Warriors and Guardians: Native Highland Trees,* Argyll Publishing, 1994.

Fischer, R., 'Sind Spitzenentladungen mitverantwortlich für Waldschäden?' *Allgemeine Forstzeitung* 13/1993.

Fischer, Rainer, *Die Abhängigkeit des Erdmagnetfeldes von der Luftelektrizität und dem Bewuchs der Kontinente,* (information sheet published by the author), 1994.

Fischer-Rizzi, Susanne, *Blätter von Bäumen,* Hugendubel, Munich 1996.

Folkard, R., *Plant-lore: Legends and Lyrics,* London 1892.

Fuhrmann, Manfred (Transl.) *Tacitus: Germania,* Reclam, Stuttgart 1995.

Gantz, Jeffrey (Transl.), *The Mabinogion,* Penguin, 1982.

Gibson, Alex, 'The Timber Circle at Sarn-y-bryn-caled, Welshpool' in Aldhouse-Green.

— *Stonehenge and Timber Circles,* Tempus Publishing, 2000.

Gibson, Alex, Burl, Aubrey & Simpson, Derek (Eds.), *Prehistoric Ritual and Religion,* Alan Sutton Publishing, Stroud 1998.

Goudsblom, Johan, *Fire and Civilization,* Penguin, 1994.

Graupe, Friedrich & Scherer, Max, *Der Mann aus dem Eis,* Goldmann, 1991.

Graves, Robert, *Greek Myth Vol. I & II,* Penguin, 1975.

— *The White Goddess,* Faber & Faber, 1999.

Green, M.J., *The Religions of Civilian Roman Britain,* British Archaeology Reports 24, 1976.

Green, M.J., *Dictionary of Celtic Myth & Legend,* Thames & Hudson, 1992.

— *Exploring the World of the Druids,* Thames & Hudson, 1997.

Grimm, Jacob, (Transl. Stallybrass, James S.), *Teutonic Myth, Vol I,* Bell, 1882.

Gwynn, Edward (Ed.), *The Metrical Dindsenchas I-V,* Hodges Figgis, Dublin 1903–35.

Hacheney, Wilfried, *Protocol of a seminar on water in Herrsching, Germany* (21–23 June, 1991), Herrsching, 1991.

— *Wasser: Ein Gast der Erde, Aquädukt,* Dingfelder Verlag, 1992.

Hart, Cyril, & Raymond, Charles, *British Trees in Colour,* Michael Joseph, 1973.

Heath, Francis George, *Tree Lore,* Charles H. Kelly, 1912.

Janik, Otto & Starosselski, Leonid B. (Eds.), 'Supernovae und Baumwachstum' in *Exakt — Exklusiv-Informationen aus Wirtschaft, Wissenschaft, Forschung und Technik in der Sowjetunion,* 5/1976, Deutsche Verlagsanstalt, Stuttgart 1976.

Johnson, Hugh, *The International Book of Trees,* Mitchell Beazley, 1973.

Jones, T. Gwynn, *Welsh Folk-Lore and Folk-Custom,* D.S. Brewer, 1979.

Julius, F.H., & Kranich, E.M., *Bäume und Planeten,* Verlag Freies Geistesleben, Stuttgart 1989.

Kelly, Fergus, 'The Old Irish Tree-List,' *Celtica II,* 107–24, 1976.

— *Early Irish Farming,* Dublin Institute for Advanced Studies, 1997.

Kluge, Friedrich, *Etymologisches Wörterbuch der deutschen Sprache,* Berlin, New York 1975.

Kneissler, Michael, 'Das letzte Geheimnis des Wassers: Es hat ein Gedächtnis,' in
    PM 3/1997, Gruner & Jahr, Munich 1997.
Kolpaktchy, Gregoire (Ed., transl.), *Egyptisches Totenbuch,* Scherz, Bern 1970.
Kranich, E.M., *Planetary Influences upon Plants,* Biodynamic Literature,
    Wyoming 1984.
Lady Gregory, *Gods and Fighting Men,* Colin Smythe, 1970.
Larousse Encyclopedia of Mythology, Chancellor Press, 1996.
Lethaby, *Architecture, Mysticism, and Myth,* London 1892
Mabinogion, see Gantz
Mannhardt, Wilhelm, *Der Baumkultus der Germanen und ihrer Nachbarstämme,*
    Mythologische Untersuchungen, Gebrüder Bornträger, Berlin 1875.
— *Antike Wald und Feldkulte aus nordeuropäischen Überlieferungen,* Gebrüder
    Bornträger, Berlin 1877.
Markale, Jean, *Die Druiden, Gesellschaft und Götter der Kelten,* Goldmann,
    Munich 1989.
Matthek, Clau & Breloer, Helge, *The Body Language of Trees,* HMSO, 1994.
Matthews, Caitlin & John, *The Encyclopedia of Celtic Wisdom,* Element, 1994.
Matthews, John (Ed.), *The Druid Source Book,* Blandford, 1996.
Mauseth, James D., *Botany: An Introduction to Plant Biology,* Jones & Bartlett
    Publishing International, 1998.
Mengel, Konrad, *Ernährung und Stoffwechsel der Pflanze,* Spektrum Akademischer
    Verlag, Heidelberg, 1991.
Milner, J. Edward, *The Tree Book: The Indispensable Guide to Tree Facts, Crafts and
    Lore,* Collins & Brown, 1992.
Mühleisen, R., *Die luftelektrischen Elemente im Grosstadtbereich,* 1953.
Murphy, Arthur (Transl.) *Tacitus: Historical Works, Vol II,.* J.M. Dent, *c.* 1915.
Parker Pearson, & M., Ramilisonina, 'Stonehenge for the Ancestors: The Stones
    Pass on the Message,' in *Antiquity* 72, 1998.
Pennar, Meirion (Transl.), *The Black Book of Carmarthen,* Llanerch, 1989.
Pennick, Nigel, *Rune Magic,* Aquarian Press, 1992.
Pfeiffer, John E., *The Emergence of Society: A Prehistory of the Establishment,*
    McGraw-Hill, New York 1978.
Philpot, J.H., *The Sacred Tree: The Tree in Religion and Myth,* Llanerch, 1994.
Plochmann, Richard, 'Mensch und Wald,' *see* Stern.
Pogacnik, Marko, *Die Erde heilen: Das Modell Türnich,* Diederichs, Munich, 1994.
Porteous, Alexander, *The Lore of the Forest: Myths and Legends,* Senate, 1996.
Rackham, Oliver, *Trees and Woodland in the British Landscape,* J.M. Dent, 1976.
— *Ancient Woodland: Its History, Vegetation and Uses in England,* Edward
    Arnold, 1980.
Rajda, V., *Electro-Diagnostics of the Health of Oak Trees,* CSAV, Czechoslovakia, 1992.
Rhys, John, *Celtic Folklore,* Clarendon Press, 1901.
Richens, R.H., *Elm,* Cambridge University Press, 1983.
Rolleston, T.W., *The Illustrated Guide to Celtic Mythology,* Studio Editions, 1993.
— *Celtic Myth,* Senate, 1994.
Roux, Francoise le, & Guyonvarch, Christian-J., *Die Druiden,* Arun, Engerda, 1996.
Schauberger, *see* Alexandersson and Coats.
Scheffer, Mechthild, *Bach Flower Therapy: Theory and Practice,* Thorsons, 1990.
Schröder, Wolfgang, 'Ändert sich der Wald, ändert sich die Tierwelt,' *see* Stern.

Shéaghdha, Nessa ní (Ed.), *Tóruigheacht Dhiarmada agus Ghráinne* [The Pursuit of Diarmuid and Grainne], Irish Text Society, Dublin 1967

Stäubli, H. Bechtold, *Handwörterbuch des deutschen Aberglaubens*, 1927.

Steiner, Rudolf, *Spiritual Foundations for the Renewal of Agriculture*, Bio-Dynamic Farming and Gardening, Kimberton, Pennsylvania 1993.

Stern, Horst, *Rettet den Wald*, Kindler, Munich 1979.

Storl, Wolf-Dieter, 'Das esoterische Baumlexikon: Weissdorn,' in *Esotera* 5/1997, Freiburg 1997.

— 'Das esoterische Baumlexikon: Linde,' in *Esotera* 7/1997, Freiburg 1997

Struss, Dieter, *Reisen in die Tiefe des Waldes: Die Geschichte der Bäume unter der Herrschaft des Menschen*, Schönberger, Munich 1986.

Tacitus, *Germania, see* Fuhrmann

— *Historical Works, see* Murphy

Tipping, Richard, 'The Form and Fate of Scotland's Woodlands,' *Proc Soc Antiq Scot*, 124 (1994), 1–54, Stirling 1994.

Trendwende, Uebel, Brigitte & Jochen F. (Eds.), Worpswede, Germany.

Trevelyan, Marie, *Folk-Lore and Folk-Stories of Wales*, Eliot Stock, 1909.

Vickery, Roy, *A Dictionary of Plant Lore*, Oxford University Press, 1995.

Warneck, Igor, *Runen-Welten*, Schirner, Darmstadt 1997.

Weinreb, F., *Die Rolle Esther*, Origo, Bern 1980.

West, Edward William (Transl.), *Pahlavi Texts, Sacred Books of the East Vol. 5*, Motilal Banarsidass, Delhi 1987.

Whipple, F.J.W., & Scrase, F.J., 'Point Discharge in the Electrical Field of the Earth,' *Geophys. Mem. Off.* No. 68, London 1936.

Whittle, A., 'Sacred Mound, Holy Rings: Silbury Hill and the West Kennet Palisade Enclosures: a Later Neolithic Complex in North Wiltshire,' *Oxbow Monograph* 74, 1997.

Wilkinson, Gerald, *A History of Britain's Trees*, Hutchinson, 1981.

Wilks, J.H., *Trees of the British Isles in History and Legend*, Frederick Muller, 1972.

Wirth, Herman, *Die heilige Urschrift der Menschheit*, Mutter Erde, Frauenberg 1979.

Yarden, L., *The Tree of Light, A Study of the Menorah*, East & West Library, 1971.

Index

Heritage of Trees
History, Culture and Symbolism

Fred Hageneder

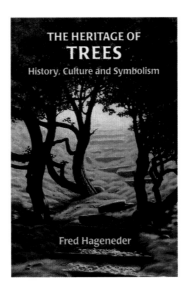

A wide-ranging study of the symbolism and cultural meaning of the tree through history, from the Cosmic Tree of antiquity to modern European, American and Asian customs and beliefs.

Many people today take the presence of trees for granted, unaware of their greater significance in stabilizing the Earth's ecology, or the veneration bestowed on them by ancient peoples.

In the companion volume, The Spirit of Trees, Fred Hageneder captivated readers with a passionate and informed account of the natural life and ecology of trees. The Heritage of Trees, extends his description of the relationship between humanity and trees down the centuries, evoking forest customs, images and meanings of the forest from the Stone Age to modern times.

www.florisbooks.co.uk

Flowforms
The Rhythmic Power of Water

John Wilkes

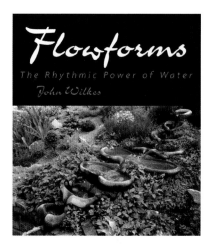

Water is not only fundamental to life but is essential for the cycles and changes in nature. John Wilkes argues that water is the universal bearer of the character we put into it. For this reason the way we treat water is of crucial importance to our health, and to the well-being of our planet.

Working with his remarkable invention, the Flowform, Wilkes has uncovered hidden secrets of the world of water, and at the same time created an artform of great beauty. His lifetime of applied research into rhythms and water, fully revealed in this book for the first time, has startling implications for such topical issues as farming and irrigation; food production and processing; water treatment and recycling; and health and cosmetic products.

This ground-breaking book is lavishly illustrated to show both the beauty of the Flowform and the wide range of its applications.

www.florisbooks.co.uk

Ecovillages

A Practical Guide to Sustainable Communities

Jan Martin Bang

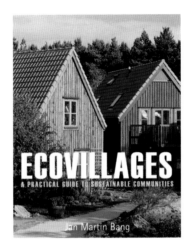

The Ecovillages movement is a worldwide network of communities which strive to integrate a supportive social environment with a low-impact way of life. Examples include Kibbutz, Camphill communities and others based on frameworks such as Permaculture.

This book explores the background and history to the Ecovillages movement, and goes on to provide a comprehensive manual for planning, establishing and maintaining a sustainable community. Issues discussed include leadership and conflict management, house design, building techniques, farming and food production, water and sewage, energy sources and alternative economics. In the final chapter, the author brings it all together in a step-by-step guide.

www.florisbooks.co.uk